"This is a bea[...]
lationships wi[...] with
animals. I will r[...] again solely to enjoy the author's
use of language—lyrical, descriptive, and direct all at
once. In some ways, it's a Southern novel—set in the
South and written by a Southerner, one who truly
knows and feels the region. But the story is univer-
sal—a couple reexamining a strained marriage, a man
and a woman looking back on their individual lives
and pondering what is next, a man and his father
struggling to reconnect after a lifetime of alienation,
and three people who love animals that are incompat-
ible with each other. In some ways, the story is tender;
in others it is terrifying. It will make you smile, but
it will also make you cry. And you will remember and
think about the characters long after you return the
novel to your bookshelf."

George Adams, *South of Little Rock*

"Terry Engel has written a wondrous novel. It's the profound romance of a man for the land, the grace of place, the sounds and smells and sweat of real people in a real out-of-town world, the not-so-well-to-do exurbs, smart people, sensitive people, thoughtful people, doing their lives justice in a place and a way we don't read about so much these days. The place is everywhere between cities and towns, the farmland, clear cut, pasture land, fields of crops that surround us all. In particular, in this case, outside of Natchez, Mississippi, up on the bluff overlooking the big river, and down in the hollows farther out of town. Natchez at Sunset is a remarkable tour de force, a disclosure of what it's like not in the cities, not on the internet 14 hours a day, not in the cool clubs or casinos or beaches, but out in the world of the cool evening dirt, in the weeds, out by the livestock, in the woods and down by a small river in these United States today. The novel is a lovely, rich, detailed, rewarding story of a not quite perfectly fitted couple rearranging them-selves and a few other favorite creatures so that the fit gets better over time. It'll please you and tease you and surprise you and, eventually, shock and sadden you, break your heart in a dozen pieces. Not the kind of thing you come across very often these days. A book worthy of being cherished."

Frederick Barthelme, *Bob the Gambler*, *Moon Deluxe*

"A rich and gripping novel with complex relationships between wolves and humans. The natural world is beautifully rendered, as are the lives of the characters. This is a Mississippi that breaks through the tired stereotypes. Excellent writing with no shortcuts."

John Henry Fleming, *Songs for the Deaf*

"Like the natural world that is so much a part of the story, this novel is beautiful, quiet, wild, tragic, and wonderful. The sense of place is palpable, and the relationships heart-wrenchingly true."

Katie Hannah, Director of University of Tennessee Press

"A patient and beautifully written story...The writing reminded me so much of Wendell Berry's, where the natural world is alive and the story sinks into the rhythm of the world around."

Kristen McCook

"Wrenching, haunting, lush, atmospheric, at times lovely, and often lonely as hell. I really enjoyed getting absorbed in this one. Everyone seemed fully imagined. Engel's love for the writing & dedication to the line shone through."

Liv Ryan, Central Arkansas Library, Little Rock

NATCHEZ AT SUNSET

NATCHEZ AT SUNSET

a novel

TERRY ENGEL

Roadrunner Press

NATCHEZ AT SUNSET
A novel
By Terry Engel

Copyright © by Terry Engel
2024

Published by
Roadrunner Press

979-8218432300 Print ISBN
979-8-218-43231-7 Ebook-ISBN

Printed in the United States of America

x ~

To Lisa, Julia Rose, and Stella

A coyote perched on top of the mailbox—a gutted carcass fitted over the metal like an envelope—looking like it had died going for the mailman's throat. Caleb coasted the pickup even with the post and turned off the motor. The mail, bound in a rubber band, lay on the edge of the road in the blackberry brambles. The engine ticked over the silence of the woods, but the bird noise slowly started back. The coyote's eyes were glazed over. The mouth had frozen in a snarl with the tongue dangling to one side. A newspaper clipping was crumpled and shoved in the coyote's mouth. Caleb leaned out the window and took the clipping and dropped it on the floor of the pickup along with the others. He reached for the nine-millimeter under the seat and ejected the clip and made sure the chamber was empty, then pushed the clip back and worked the slide to load it. He thumbed down the hammer and lay the gun on the seat.

Flies buzzed the coyote's mottled flanks and open mouth and a line of ants trooped up the post, disappearing inside the body cavity. The dense pine woods that formed a barrier between his house and the road were dark and quiet. The right of way on either side of the road was grown up in sumac and blackberry choked in road dust from a dry summer.

He cranked the truck and idled the pickup down the road. A quarter mile past the narrow slash in the pines that was his driveway, he turned onto a fire road carpeted with pine needles and drove another couple hundred yards along a ridge before parking. Caleb plucked his sweat-soaked shirt off his back and enjoyed the brief cool. The air was heavy under the deep shade of the thick canopy of pines and smelled of turpentine and needle mulch. A squirrel barked a few times and then moved away through the tree limbs. He could just make out the shape of the house, a boxy two story, in a small clearing of brown grass. Jessica's Subaru was parked in front. Flashes from her arc welder splashed from the dark interior of the Quonset hut where he parked his equipment.

Caleb tucked the pistol in his belt in the small of his back and walked along the ridge behind the house, paralleling the trail that ran from the house through the woods to the pen, which he had built above Black Creek so the wolves would get the breeze. He practiced walking silently across the pine needle floor, watching for movement and listening for sound. Just out of view of the pen, Caleb dropped to his hands and knees, and crawled through the brush.

The eight-foot chain link enclosed an acre of bottomland forest, huge old hardwoods that had shaded out the understory, leaving the forest floor parklike. Mounds marked where the wolves had dug dens. The two wolves, either excited by the coyote scent or the sound of Caleb's approach, padded figure eights around the clearing behind the gate. The male, Max, stopped pacing and craned his neck toward the sky, caught Caleb's scent, and stared at his hiding place in the undergrowth. The female, Lulu, had her back to the male, but without any visual signal passing between the wolves, she turned and stared at Caleb's spot.

Every day he tried to sneak up on the wolves, varying his approach, trying different times of day, spraying himself with aerosols ordered from hunting catalogs that promised to mask his scent. He wanted to spy on them, but it was impossible. He knew the wolves communicated with sounds his ears couldn't register, but at times it seemed that they could not only read each other's, but his mind as well.

He watched them until they grew tired of staring at him and resumed pacing. Max and Lulu moved like water in a slowly swirling eddy, intent on their own business, ears cocked to every sound.

Caleb picked up the bundle of mail and tossed it in the cab and pulled his leather gloves off the dash. The coyote came off the mailbox reluctantly. The carcass had stiffened and the blood dried to the metal. The red flag bent out beneath the animal, and Caleb couldn't help but think about the black man he and his father had found while hunting deer, years ago, when Caleb was still a boy and he and his father still hunted together. The man was from the coast, Biloxi or Pas Christian, and no one had ever been able to explain what he was doing fifty miles north. He had been beaten and strapped naked across the hood of a car abandoned on a fire road in the national forest that bordered Hubert's land, with the engine running long enough to run out of gas. When Caleb and Hubert found him, he was unconscious.

Caleb shook the image out of his mind and tried to focus on the coyote, lean and covered with fleas and ticks and bare skin where mange had eaten away the fur. Caleb's stomach turned, his usual reaction to handling dead animals. An image of his father standing off to the side, shaking his head at his squeamishness, played through his mind. He dropped the coyote on the ground and looked it over. There was a bullet wound just behind the front shoulder and another in the hindquarters. Caleb looped a rope around the animal and attached the other end to the bumper so the scent wouldn't stain his truck. The coyote's guts were stuffed inside the mailbox, and he scraped them into a garbage bag. As he dragged the coyote down the road he thought that he would have to get back and clean the mailbox before Jessica checked the mail.

Hubert's pickup came on in the distance, crowding the middle. The old man stopped and rolled down his window, pushing his straw cowboy hat back on his head. Caleb went around him, barely slowing. He raised one finger off the wheel in a wave and stared straight ahead. In the side mirror he watched Hubert stick his head out the window and stare at the carcass raising dust at the end of the rope.

After a mile Caleb turned down an old forest service fire road. Branches lashed the open windows. Sunlight filtered through the canopy overhead and reflected off the windshield and the junk that lined the road: White enameled appliances riddled with bullet holes, rusted steel drums and five gallon herbicide cans, a sofa with foam leaking from a dozen holes in the fabric, tin cans and rotting plastic garbage bags, soiled disposable diapers, faded cardboard beer cartons, empty bottles and cans, cigarette butts, soiled clothes, scorched fire rings —all covered with a thin layer of leaf and pine needle mulch, garnished with poison ivy and pine cones and lacy ferns. The road ended beside an eroded red clay gulch fifty feet deep. A couple of wrecked cars had been driven or pushed over the edge and lay at the bottom beside a pool of water surrounded by more trash. Caleb untied the rope from the bumper and dragged the coyote to the edge. He tossed the bag of guts into the pool and rolled the animal over the edge with the toe of his boot. It slid down the bank and splashed in the pool. The garbage bag floated across the rippling water and grounded at the far end. He sat on the bank and dangled his legs over the edge, too tired of the threats to feel anger. It was more just an overwhelming sadness that people had to be so mean. The water on the surface of the pool stilled and the sediment cloud roiled by the coyote dissipated. Other than the wrecked cars and the garbage, the gulch was a pretty place. It was quiet during the week, when the teenagers did their drinking in town, and deer and turkey and other animals came down to the water to drink at night. The red clay had eroded into sharp fins and spires, and the walls of the gulch were laced with white, blue, and green striations.

Back in the pickup, he took the long way home, coming out on the highway and then dropping down to the big river, the Neshoba, below where Black Creek fed into it. He leaned over the wheel so the wind would dry the back of his shirt. He found himself tailgating an old Dodge Ram flying frayed-end flags from whip antennas attached to the cab: a Thin Blue Line American on the left, and a Confederate battle flag on the right. The rear window of the cab sported a gun rack with a couple of assault rifles with banana clips. He slowed down to give the truck room.

When he got to the river he crossed the bridge and parked at the boat ramp. The river was a hundred yards wide here, but low and clear. Fifty miles downstream it emptied into the Gulf of Mexico. The Fish and Game sign warning against eating more than four ounces of catfish a month had been shot up and weathered to the point it was safe to ignore, although no one had ever paid attention to it when the lettering was fresh and the discovery of dioxin in the river, discharge from the pulp mill upstream, was still news. Even before the state stopped monitoring the mills, Indian River Pulp and Paper had been dumping hydrogen sulfide and dioxin into the water. Caleb had written about the Environmental Defense Fund's call to close the river to commercial and recreational fishing in the *Three Rivers Times*. For a while it was big news, bringing in environmental activists to protest the state's environmental record.

There had been clashes between "outside agitators" and the locals outside the mill, windshields of out-of-state cars smashed at motels, death threats. Caleb's articles had pissed off everyone from the Missionary Baptists to the Ku Klux Klan. When the newspaper began losing advertising, he was fired "for his personal safety." Indian River kept on dumping. The river still ran clear and locals and commercial fishermen still fished, and the only dangers anyone cared about were the water moccasins or alligators sunning on sandbars.

The pickup Caleb had followed earlier came back. It did a slow turn through the boat launch parking lot. Caleb could feel the driver and his passenger looking him over. They parked up by the road for a few minutes, then drove slowly toward Caleb's truck, turning and backing down the ramp. The driver looked over at Caleb and nodded, but Caleb didn't know him. He backed up to the water's edge and the two men got out, pulling their AR 15s off the gun rack and walking to the back of the truck. The passenger gave Caleb a long look before laying his gun down in the bed. He opened the tailgate and grabbed a milk jug and dipped it in the water, filling it just enough to toss it out in the river fifty or sixty feet. The driver levered a round into his rifle and cut loose, four or five bursts, emptying the clip while the water exploded around the milk jug and it disintegrated. The driver turned to Caleb, the gun cradled loosely in his hands.

Caleb leaned against a sawhorse and watched Jessica bend over her work, a welded sculpture she called "Natchez at Sunset." He looked away from the white light of the welding rod touching metal. The piece was part of the show she planned for the university at the beginning of the year. It was the size of a pickup and, only half completed, already weighed over a ton. The riverbed and the bluff that Natchez perched on were layered sections of steel plate, and the cloud and sky backdrop were copper sheet colored with heat and chemicals to bring out the oranges, pinks, and violets of a Mississippi river sunset lighting the eastern bank. Jessica had welded an A-frame mast to Caleb's bull-dozer so they could use the winch to lift the piece onto the trailer. They hadn't yet worked out a plan for unloading the sculpture at the university.

Jessica ejected the nub of smoking welding rod and reached into her leather apron for another. As she tilted the hood back on her head and leaned over to adjust the voltage on the arc welder, she saw him, frowned, and snapped her head, shutting the hood again. She bent back over the piece, light flashing, and tiny particles of molten steel showering the ground. The generator on the welder revved as Jessica pulled amps, the steel sizzled under the flow and fusion of electrons, and the workshop filled with bitter smoke. It was the smell of poorly lighted machine shops and garages that Caleb had grown up around—a smell as familiar as diesel smoke and hydraulic fluid and oil absorbent, which, along with the sound of hammered metal and cursing, the heft of ball-peen hammers and socket wrenches, and the vibration of heavy equipment straining against a load, still thrilled the boy inside of him.

The smell was Jessica's smell, as distinctive as any perfume. When she ejected the last rod and cut the generator, the workshop fell silent and the fumes drifted away. She pulled off her heavy leather gloves, removed the hood and bandana and shook out her sweat-damp hair. She picked up a hammer and stared at the sculpture.

She was forty-two. Tall. Strong. A woman who worked with her hands and muscles, she didn't worry about the grime under her fingernails. A few wrinkles around her eyes when she smiled, but pretty. A woman whose father had built the Alaska Pipeline, her childhood dream, but she had gone there to work after high school and had come back disappointed. Her father helped her get on at the shipyard in Pascagoula, and she made master welder, just like him, fusing straight seams and breathing through respirators in the holds of newborn ships. When the shipyards shut down and the jobs moved to China, she'd gone to New Orleans and made a living creating star, moon, and sun wind chimes; bird baths; and sundials. She did an apprenticeship with an artist who cast bronze gongs and bells, which they sold in the French Market to Mardi Gras tourists. It was never clear to Caleb to what degree she and the artist had been lovers. She was vague on the subject, just as she was vague on what had happened— or didn't happen—in Alaska, and he didn't pry. He often wondered about who had taken all those pictures of her at nineteen, when she was living in someone's

Volkswagen van and posing under the Alaska Pipeline. Nevertheless, she'd left New Orleans with what she could fit in a Subaru and had ended up in DeSoto, where she'd been commissioned by the alumni association at the university to do a sculpture. She produced a curved steel ladder that cast a shadow like a soaring golden eagle, the school's mascot. The university had kept her on to teach in the art department, where she'd been for twelve years, working her way up from part time instructor to artist in residence.

A year or two after she got on with the university, Caleb met her when he covered an exhibit for the *Three Rivers*. Caleb hadn't expected Jessica. She looked like she'd walked off a construction yard, with her scuffed steel-toed boots, ragged jeans, and flannel shirt. She'd told him they could meet behind the art department, where he found her unloading a flatbed of scrap metal with a truck-mounted knuckle boom she'd borrowed from landscaping. She was too busy to answer his questions, so he stepped in to rig the choker cable around a bundle of metal and tag the load so she wouldn't have to keep climbing down from the controls. After they finished they sat on the bed of the truck and talked, then made a date for beers later that evening. The night ended with Caleb driving her down to his land, where they'd walked for hours and ended the night sitting on a sandbar beside Black Creek. Not long after they'd married.

Caleb tossed the packet of mail on the workbench in front of her. She turned to him, finally, dangling the hammer. "There's a letter there from an adoption agency," Caleb said.

"China?"

Jessica glanced at the packet of mail. She placed the hammer on the bench and picked up a mill file and ran it across the edge of the sculpture.

"What's it say?" she asked.

"I didn't read it. It's not addressed to me."

"It's your business too."

"It was my business when we were talking to those people in Russia. It was my business when we found Lacey."

Jessica reacted to the name, a flash of pain that she covered quickly. "It's just another option," Jessica said. She picked up the mail and thumbed through it until she found the letter.

"Go ahead," Caleb said.

He waited on her. The way her hands shook as she handled the letter was almost enough to forgive her. He walked to the door of the shop hoping for a breeze, but the heat only intensified with the daylight. After a minute he turned around.

"Well?"

"Same story. It's a lot of money we don't have. Air fares, legal fees, interviews. No guarantees. A real long shot."

"You knew that already."

She tossed the letter away. She started past him but he grabbed her by the hand and pulled her into his arms. He buried his face in her neck, breathing her in. She pulled away and rubbed at her eyes, smearing her face with the black oxidation of the metal. She pulled the pistol out of his belt.

"What's wrong?" "Nothing's wrong."

Jessica set the pistol on the bench. "Max and Lulu were acting strange earlier, pacing and howling. They wouldn't come to me."

"Maybe it's the heat."

"No," she said, running her fingers over the ridges of the file. "It's been too quiet out here today. No birds, no traffic on the road. It's like everything's been spooked."

"I don't know." He nodded toward the sculpture. "Are you done for the day?"

"Yeah," she said, taking off her apron and switching off the power to the welder.

Caleb tucked the pistol into his belt. She didn't say anything else. He held Jessica's hand as they walked down the trail to the wolf pen, conscious of the weight of the gun. Jessica started to say something but swallowed it. Caleb adjusted the gun so it rode better.

Lulu was waiting. She lay by the gate, her head resting on her forelegs. Max lay hidden somewhere in the undergrowth. Lulu stood as they entered the pen, wagging her tail and fawning for Jessica. She knelt by Lulu. The wolf rolled over and let Jessica rub the coarse fur of her belly, perhaps fifteen seconds, before she tired of being touched and her natural wariness took over.

"Wise old girl," Jessica said.

Of the two, Lulu was the gentler and more dependable. She weighed a hundred pounds and had sharp gray and white markings, with a little patch of black on her throat. Max was harder to control. His dark gray coat was frosted with black, and he weighed a hundred and thirty. He could place his front paws on Caleb's shoulders and look him in the eye. Caleb caught a glimpse of Max for just a second, peering over a fallen log thirty yards away. A moment later he peeked from behind a pine tree on the opposite side of the clearing. The wolf disappeared again and reappeared a few steps closer, watching them from the cover of a muscadine

vine. When he'd finally stalked his way close enough
Max leaped at Caleb, nipping at his rear as he flew past.
The wolf had long ago ripped the back pants pockets
off of all Caleb's jeans, so that he'd stopped wearing
new clothes when he came to the pen. He didn't think
that Max would ever hurt him, but sometimes, when
he felt the power of those jaws, Caleb imagined Max
ripping away a chunk of flesh and retreating to the far
side of the pen to gobble it down.

When Max tired of nipping at Caleb he rushed at
Lulu and bowled her over. When the female recovered,
he nipped at Lulu's feet, cutting her away from Jessica
like a dog herding sheep. Max returned to Jessica and
reared up and placed his paws on her shoulders, buckling her a little under his weight. He nibbled and licked
at her nose. Caleb harnessed Lulu and attached the
leash. She stood at the gate, patient, but Max refused
to stand still and he pulled and bullied against the
harness.

They walked along the sandy trail above the creek.
The dark, tannin-stained water flowed over gravel
shoals and logs. In places the water was just a few
inches deep and glowed golden above the gravel and
sand and leaves lining the bottom. The wolves started
and stopped, freezing at every slight motion, whether
a falling leaf or a squirrel scampering through the
tree canopy. They sniffed at tree trunks and bushes,
and Max lifted his leg to mark territory. Their noses
trembled when the wind shifted and brought something new.

The wolves crossed and re-crossed the trail, circled
and wrapped Caleb and Jessica's legs in the leashes
and crossed each other's leashes, sometimes jerking

them off their feet lunging after mice or startled arma-
dillos and opossums.

Caleb had envisioned letting the wolves roam, but
once off the leash there was no guarantee they would
come back. Max had disappeared for two days when
he was about six months old, only coming back out of
loneliness for Lulu. Caleb suspected that raising them
in captivity had made them unsuitable for the wild.
But the pen still provided cover for Max's stalking
game. They visited the creek every day, and often at
night. And the wolves taught him to see. The once invisible outline of a rattlesnake along the path, or a deer
bedded in tall grass, now stood out. He was learning
to discern motion from stillness, to test the wind for
what it might tell him, to notice the way light painted
an object at different times of the day and year.

They stopped at a wide gravel and sand bar where
the river made a bend and cypress trees buttressed by
knobby knees formed a tiny green island in the main
channel. They transferred the wolves from the leashes
to long logging chains secured to a river birch, and the
wolves waded into the current and began to drink. The
chains were long enough that the wolves could wade
the creek but couldn't climb the opposite bank.

Caleb brushed the sand off a piece of driftwood
and placed the gun pointing away from the water. He
removed his sweaty clothes as he watched Jessica undress. She was a few inches shorter than him, and like
Caleb, she had added a little weight with age. She had
an honest look, direct. They walked along the sand
bar out of range of Max's clawing feet and waded into
the water. Caleb crouched in the coolness and Jessica
nestled in front of him. He listened for the sound of
aluminum canoes banging into gravel bars upstream,

though it was unlikely with the creek this low and the university empty for the summer.

"If you did have a reason for carrying your gun today, you'd tell me, wouldn't you?"

He wrapped his arms around her and cupped her breasts. "Sure."

"You're lying," she said, and pulled his hands to her stomach and held them there. She scooped a handful of gravel off the creek bed and tossed the pebbles one at a time. "Well?"

"Somebody killed a coyote and left it on our mailbox."

"Left it on the mailbox?"

"Like a hood ornament."

Jessica pulled out another handful of gravel. "What do you think we ought to do about it?"

"I don't know," Caleb said. "Nothing, I guess."

"Nothing?"

"What do you want me to do?"

"Call the sheriff."

"They haven't done anything about the letters. They won't do anything about this."

Jessica twisted a little to look at him.

"I don't think they'll come back," Caleb said. "I'm not writing anymore." He watched the wolves. Lulu lay at the far end of the sandbar, resting her head on her forelegs, body half in the creek, cooling down. "This heat will drive anyone crazy."

Jessica stood and waded deeper into the river and Caleb watched her go. She leaned back and dipped her hair in the water, then slid back and floated. He stared at her breasts and felt the stirring of an erection, but he didn't follow. It had been a while since she had wanted him to.

It felt like a lazy Sunday afternoon. The grass tall and golden in the late summer heat. Horseflies buzzed grazing cattle and dove and meadowlark called from the trees. Crows racketed overhead. One cow looked up from feeding and eyed the tree line and bawled in protest. The coyote crossed the open pasture in an easy lope, parting the cattle like a boat parting smooth water. Just before it reached the tree line a rifle shot cut the stillness. The coyote tumbled into a headlong somersault and lay still, panting as its life ebbed away. Caleb felt the burning in his shoulder and then the paralysis as his lungs froze. He gasped for breath, but only dryness came. The grass moved with a light wind. A man approached slowly, stopped, prodded him with the muzzle of a rifle, nudged him with the toe of his boot. Caleb's eyes rolled up the human above him, following the Redwing boots up the jean clad legs, up the flannel shirt to the face—his own face. He looked down at the coyote as its eyes glazed over.

A distant ringing and Jessica mumbled something and rolled over in her sleep, shaking the bed. Caleb sat up and looked at his phone on the nightstand. The caller ID didn't recognize the number. It went to voicemail several times before whoever was calling gave up. He listened to Jessica's breathing deepen to a light snore. The sheets and pillowcases were hot and damp with sweat and his legs felt restless. Before the dream he had lain awake, his mind going here and there. Trying not to wake Jessica, he reached for his

T-shirt on the floor, wiped the sweat from his back, and stood up.

The alarm showed 2:10. Caleb walked to the window but there was no breeze. Nothing but pine shadows from the weak moon. He walked downstairs to the den. In the kitchen he fixed a glass of ice water and went out onto the deck. The thermometer still hung above eighty and it wouldn't drop until just before daylight. Lulu gave a long howl that carried through the woods. Late at night, the sound still spooked him a little.

The coyote dream was real enough that he had been glad the phone had rung him awake. Most of his dreams he couldn't connect with anything real. The exception was when he dreamed about the black man tied to a car.

There was nothing on TV that late. Preaching on one channel and weather radar on the other, but Caleb went back to the den and turned on the set, second guessing his decision to let the satellite subscription drop after the last election. The television preacher sat in a rocking chair with an open bible on his lap, nothing more than a prop, since he never looked at it when he spoke. His gray eyes bored into his imagined audience. A river mural had been painted on the set behind the man, like the scene that old country churches used above the baptistery: the river Jordan inviting the lost to wash away their sins in baptism. It was almost the same mural Caleb had spent countless hours wishing himself into as a child, as he sat straight-backed against the bare oak pew, dressed in black suit and white shirt with a clip-on tie digging into his throat, afraid to squirm or even pull the too tight collar away for fear of Hubert dragging him up the aisle to the front steps for a whipping. From the earliest Caleb could remember, Hubert and his mother went to church every Sunday morning and evening for worship and preaching, and every Wednesday night for Bible study and singing. Hubert tolerated no fool-ishness in church, and while other kids drew stick men on paper or even sprawled along the pew with their heads in their mothers' laps, Caleb feigned per-fect attention to the preacher sweating at the pulpit. Salvation had been that mural and the cooling water it promised. Caleb had spent countless sermons scan-ning every inch of that river. He hung a rope on a tree that leaned out over the water, and he imagined giant catfish lurking in the deep pools. Jesus had been bap-tized in that water and the spirit of God descended on him in the form of a dove. It was years later, as an adult, that it occurred to Caleb that the mural featured a white-tail deer drinking at the foot of cypress trees draped with Spanish moss, a lovely, delicate, parasitic plant better suited to Mississippi than to Israel.

As an adult, Caleb went to church less and less, until finally, he got sick of all the people using Chris-tianity as a weapon and stayed away for good. Still, there was something comforting about listening to the rhythm of the preacher's voice rolling out those worn out phrases when the house was so dark and still.

Hubert never questioned his beliefs, and with that confidence came the strength to look down on every other waking creature in the world. Hubert slept the deep contented sleep of the justified, never feeling lonely or unsure of himself, or feeling anything other than contempt, masked as pity, for anyone who didn't name Jesus. Any non-believer was either hopelessly ignorant or embraced in a conspiracy to destroy the world. Caleb had once been that sure himself.

As the television preacher wrapped up his sermon the scene changed to people inside a church singing "The Old Rugged Cross." Caleb couldn't hear that song without remembering the Gospel meetings of his childhood, twice a year, beginning on Sunday morning and stretching the week, every night through Friday night. The purpose was to spark revival within the church and convert the lost outside the church. During the day children and teenagers went door-knocking in neighborhoods, handing out religious tracts and invitations to the meeting that night. Success of the meeting was gauged by attendance and responses. Whenever Caleb heard the song, it never failed to draw him back into all those nights in a packed church following an hour-long sermon with images of Hell-fire and eternal suffering and sleepless or nightmare filled nights. The sermons always ended with an "invitation" song, where the audience was invited to walk to the front of the auditorium and ask to be baptized or request forgiveness for public sin. The closer it got to Friday night, the preacher would keep them singing until someone broke and came forward. Sometimes the song was "Old Rugged Cross," or "Bring Christ your Broken Life," but more often it was "Just as I Am"—all six verses, with the occasional verse almost whispered. The power of two-hundred voices whispering felt like it would shatter the stained-glass windows. It was a sound designed to prick the hardest heart. Sometimes, the preacher would interrupt the song leader between verses: "I know there's at least one person in this audience with a heavy heart this evening, someone who needs to come forward and ask for forgiveness. I wouldn't feel right leaving here without singing at least one more verse of that sweet old song."

Caleb remembered singing "Just as I Am" for twenty or thirty minutes some nights, with the preacher keeping soft time with the palm of his hand on the worn leather face of his Bible. Once they'd had a week-long Gospel meeting where the visiting preacher held his Bible over his head during the invitation, the text held open to the audience, as if the words could reach out and pull the guilty forward. Caleb had been baptized already, a couple of years at least, but he stood in the audience that day, eleven or twelve years old, innocent of anything but being a child, fighting with himself not to answer the preacher's call. There was no good reason to go forward, but the weight of the words pulled like a magnet:

> "Just as I am, without one plea,
> but that Thy blood was shed for me,
> and that Thou bid'st me come to Thee,
> Oh Lamb of God I come, I come."

Verse after verse, and sometimes they'd sing the last verse over and over, or sometimes just start the song over again. Every few verses the preacher would break in to preach a little more.

Caleb broke. He'd worked his way to the end of the pew, not caring if he stepped on feet or tangled legs, and stumbled down the aisle as everyone looked up from their song books, relieved that someone had given in and they could go home soon. He walked down the aisle, all the long way to the front, into the arms of the preacher, crying like a child who can't stop once he starts, more scared than hurt. Hubert and his mother had followed Caleb to the front and sat one on each side while the preacher kneeled before him and listened to his teary confession. Caleb blurted something about wanting to rededicate his life and show others Jesus through his life, and he had cried through the preacher's speech about "tender hearts" and the prayer that followed, but when he sneaked a look at his father's face during the prayer, Hubert stared down at him, angry.

That was just one of the times Caleb had been drawn to the front of the church, pulled forward by some sin he couldn't name, although the frequency diminished when he became a teenager and stopped before high school ended. Each time, Caleb had felt relieved to be forgiven. It wasn't until years later, after much reflection and watching similar conversion scenes played out dozens of times, that he began to be first embarrassed, then angered for those people coaxed to the front. He hadn't been guilty of anything other than a weakness for not disappointing all those preachers who, he imagined, kept tally marks in the inside cover of their Bibles, one column for baptisms and another for public confessions of sin.

As he had grown older and thought about it more, Caleb began to suspect that his father hadn't been angered over some sin his son had committed, nor was he relieved that Caleb had chosen to rededicate himself to Jesus. Caleb decided it was shame Hubert felt. Shame that his son had been so weak as to have to prostrate himself before the rest of the congregation.

Earlier that evening, Jessica had insisted on being shown the mailbox. They had walked out to the road at dusk with a gallon jug of water. She had stared at the box as he described the coyote again, and Caleb knew she was imagining Lulu stretched over the bare metal. Jessica looked at him and waited a long time, but Caleb hadn't known what to say. She had turned and walked back to the house without saying anything while Caleb dug the toe of his boot into the gravel. He should have been able to tell her something about the coyote that would have made her feel better, and he knew that the coyote was going to hang on that box between them.

After the television preacher signed off with a call for donations, Caleb turned off the set and went back to bed. A light breeze filtered through the screen. Jessica rolled over as Caleb pulled up the sheet.

"Where've you been?" she asked. Her voice was thick. "Watching the preacher."

"We ought to get the satellite hooked up again. Two stations."

"At least one of them is educational," Caleb said. He wrapped an arm around Jessica's waist and nestled in behind her. "It's public now. They don't call it educational anymore." She lifted his arm and slid across the bed, closer to the window.

Hubert sat in the easy chair in his den and let the gray television light and the voice of the preacher wash over him. He gripped the arm rests of the chair with both hands and held on like he was bracing himself in a pickup bouncing through deep ruts. Everything in the room was old and reminded him of his wife, nearly thirty years dead. The pictures of their life together faced him, still arranged the way she had left them before the last trip to the hospital, the doilies covering the furniture unraveling in the night, and the furniture puffing tiny dust clouds when he eased himself down at the end of the day.

He tried to focus on what the preacher was saying as he reached for his tobacco and papers. His hands shook as he tapped out a line of tobacco into the folded paper, and his tongue wet the paper so that it tore and the cigarette disintegrated in his hands. He dropped the makings into a fruit jar so he could use them later, when his hands weren't shaking so bad. The wolves' howling had gotten him out of bed for the second time that night. Too many nights Caleb and Jessica walked the wolves all over the country. Some nights they only went as far as the river; some nights he listened and tracked them across the river and into the big clear-cut hills on the paper company land. Earlier in the evening the wolves had woken him, and for some reason he hadn't been able to track them. He'd gotten dressed and driven the circuit of his pastures, counting cattle. The moon was full and it was easy to count from a great distance. Still unsatisfied, he had parked and walked down to the river and up the trail to Caleb's sand bar. From there he crept along the path to the wolf pen. He knew the path because he often went to look at the wolves at night. The animals never exposed themselves, but they were there, somewhere in the shadows cast by logs and trees in the bright moonlight. He knew once his mind penned the wolves it would be easier to sleep.

But even that wouldn't let Hubert sleep. He couldn't get out of his mind what Doctor Pennington had told him earlier in the day. "We found a spot on your lungs. It could be malignant. We'll need to do more tests." The doctor talked and talked, as if he could take back the bad news if he kept talking. He said medicine had come a long way in the past few years. What they knew about fighting cancer when Elizabeth died was like the dark ages. There were new drugs, new treatments. Aggressive treatments. The worst thing was to give up without a fight.

"Just because I don't want you sticking any needles in me don't mean I'm giving up." Hubert said. She had melted away right before his eyes. The treatments had left her so weak the women from church had had to come and do for her.

The doctor looked at his chart like he thought the answer might be there. "Do you have any family that can help you talk through some of the decisions?"

"A son. It ain't his decision."

"Well, you might want to talk your options over once we know more. It's good to have someone to wait with you while we're running the tests. This affects other people." He paused, flipped a page on his clipboard. "It's something that doesn't need to wait."

Hubert nodded.

Pennington took off his glasses and rubbed at his eyes. "The nurse is going to come in with some literature for you to look over. Instructions. Any other questions?"

Hubert waved him off. Doctor Pennington touched Hubert's shoulder and left the room.

Needles and tubes. Needles and tubes sticking out of him, the slow chemical poison working through his veins, killing him just as sure as the cancer. Maybe quicker.

Hubert still had dreams about his wife's gray face, her labored breathing through the last night, the preacher reading the Psalms over and over. The sick look on Caleb's face as he looked up as Hubert walked into the waiting room, hoping for good news, wanting so desperately to be there with his mother at the end. Hubert knew now that he had been wrong to keep the boy out. It had been wrong to try and shield him from death that way. It had been wrong to forbid the boy's tears at the funeral as well. I don't expect he'll cry that much for me, Hubert thought.

He'd wanted to tell Caleb about the doctor, earlier that day, when he'd seen the boy dragging that coyote down the road behind his pickup. He needed to tell somebody, and he'd gotten his hopes up for a moment, seeing that coyote raising dust, so hopeful that he'd even forgotten the cancer for a minute. But then Caleb had driven on past, barely raising a finger off the wheel to acknowledge him, and the wolf at the end of the rope wasn't a wolf at all. Just a damn coyote. Hubert had wondered about that. What Caleb was doing with a coyote? The only good thing about the wolves was that they kept the coyotes away. No coyote was foolish enough to cross a wolf's territory, even if the wolves did live in a cage. Their scent must be everywhere in this bottom. But Caleb had driven past, leaving Hubert to sit in the middle of the road and wonder, leaving him with cancer on his lungs and no one to talk to.

He had talked to Elizabeth at first, after the funeral and for a good number of years afterward. He imagined her sitting in her chair, listening to him talk with that peaceful expression on her face, after Caleb went to bed. He told her everything. How she was not to worry because he was making sure the boy was brought up right. He had kept on with the church, and made sure Caleb got there for Sunday school and preaching and Wednesday night Bible study as well. Made sure the boy wore a suit and tie and had his shoes polished. Made the boy memorize a Bible verse every day. But after Caleb grew up he'd quit the church, and no amount of preaching or threatening had brought him back. Hubert kept right on going, three times a week, but he knew that he had quit the church just as much as Caleb. It had changed. Everything was feeling good about yourself. It was okay with God if you sinned a little—go ahead and do what feels good, don't worry about breaking His laws. God wanted everyone; God forgave everyone, no matter how much they sinned. Even the homosexuals and atheists. He wondered how God could want him anymore.

When the preaching ended Hubert turned off the set and turned on the lamp beside his chair. He reached for the fruit jar beside him. His hands had quit shaking and he got the cigarette rolled. He struck a match and lit the end. The paper flared and dropped glowing shards into his lap. He brushed them to the floor and reached over for the Bible and turned to the book of *Job*. He smoked the cigarette until it was a nub, then began to read.

Jessica listened to Caleb's steady breathing. He had been up in the night, so he'd probably sleep for another hour or two, at least until Lulu and Max marked the passing of darkness with a pack howl. She slipped out of bed and into jeans, t-shirt, and sandals. Caleb stirred before she could get to the door.

"Up early," he said.

"I need to go in, check my mail. Work on a few things," she said. "I'll call you later." She slipped out the door before he could say anything else.

Downstairs she made coffee and leaned against the counter while it brewed. The paneled walls and dark stained cabinets resisted the light replacing the darkness. Although clean enough, the house was no longer new, and the walls held ten years' worth of scratches and the hollow-core doors were dented. The wallpaper border below the ceiling peeled in places. The cabinet hinges squeaked and the cabinets overflowed with the accumulation of ten years of marriage, so she could never find what she was looking for without moving at least three other things. Together, she and Caleb had worked their way through three or four sets of tea glasses and dishes, so nothing matched when they sat down to eat. Their pots and pans and other utensils were an eclectic mess, with beaten up pieces from before the marriage that had been added to as the need arose. No amount of mopping could make the linoleum floor look clean again. The kitchen was dated. She wondered what replacing everything with stainless steel would cost. She wondered if it would even make a difference in how she felt.

Jessica didn't know how two people could live so hard that it aged a house in such a short time. They weren't rough people, but they didn't pretend to live in a museum either. The house had been a dream when they began planning and building it together. Every day after work and all day Saturday and Sunday they framed, roofed, wired and plumbed, hung drywall and laid linoleum and carpet, installed appliances. It was a solid, well-built house. She had thought about where the kids would sleep and play, and where she and Caleb would go to get away from the kids. They had built the biggest house they could afford at the time, and now it seemed small and dingy, not even big enough for the two of them, let alone children they would never have. The house had aged, slowly and almost imperceptibly, like she and Caleb had aged, and now she was forty-two and living in a house that she would glance at if passing on the road, but not bother to look at again.

When the coffee finished Jessica poured a cup to take with her. The rest of the pot went into her battered Stanley thermos. The sun was up and the day already growing hot as she walked down to the wolf pen. The wolves stood at the gate, waiting for her, just like every morning. Max dropped back into the morning shadows to play a game of hide and seek as Jessica worked the latch. She cooed at Lulu, who sat back from the gate, wary and unsure. She knelt and let the wolf approach. It still put Jessica off some mornings, how cautious Lulu could be, even after two years. The night wildness sometimes took the whole morning to wear off. Eventually the female would work her way up to Jessica and allow her to scratch her ears, if only for a couple of

minutes. Max almost never came to her, especially in
the mornings. If he bothered with Jessica or Caleb at all,
it was only to be harnessed, and then it was only in the
afternoons when Max would accept the harness. After
a few minutes of scratching, Lulu slunk off into the
woods. Jessica stood and brushed dirt from her knees.
As she walked to her car she analyzed the meeting for
any sign of improvement in Lulu's acceptance, but she
had to admit that she couldn't find anything.

In the Subaru she drove without thinking, enjoying the cool air flowing through the windows and tangling her hair, the sound of gravel crunching under her
tires and pinging the bottom of the car. Steering with
one knee, she twisted the pour-through spout on her
thermos and refilled her coffee cup and placed it in
the cup-holder on the dash. The once green finish on
the thermos had been scratched and dented and rolled
on floorboards and across the holds of ships so much
that it had worn to silver, but the steel was sound and
it kept the coffee so warm that it still steamed when
she had the last cup late in the afternoon. She carried
the thermos to work, to school, religiously, just as she
had every day at the shipyard and along every mile of
the Alaska Highway. She liked the weight of it and the
dull shine of the stainless steel interior that smelled
of coffee even after scalding with hot water. It was
seamless, a perfect weld. It reminded her of where she
came from on days when she stood in front of a class
and wondered.

She sipped at her coffee and watched the morning
take shape. The sky to the east flowered from a pale
rosy glow into a faint blue. Every so often the woods
drew away from the road to reveal a clear cut with a
mobile home or a small rundown house surrounded

by the junk country people never bothered to throw away. Poor Man's Flags were propped in about every other yard. Made out of shipping pallets, the flags were painted to look like Confederate battle flags, the original Betsy Ross American flag, or the rattlesnake under the motto "Don't Tread on Me." Lately she was seeing the Mississippi state outline painted in the stars and bars pattern.

She had come to a crossroads without realizing the time for a decision was approaching. She knew she would never regret Caleb. She was sure of his love, and she knew that she would always love him, but for some reason that no longer seemed like enough. She had loved her life for a while, and she had thought the wolves would make a difference. They had for a while. The woods were quiet, Caleb was steady and thoughtful, and the wolves were a magic that no other experience could equal. Where else could she walk through the night and feel two animals flow silently beside her like ghosts asking questions that could never be answered? No matter how much she tried to convince herself to the contrary, she knew she would never be happy without a child. The desire was palpable, overwhelming, like the fury she felt when she saw an asshole mistreat a dog. Nothing she said to herself was enough to overcome the disappointment and emptiness of not having a child of her own. It made her angry that Caleb had moved on, and she sometimes wondered if he had only been going along with her to make her happy. Maybe he was just as glad that there wouldn't be any children to complicate things, especially if the marriage kept heading south. He just went about his business no matter what happened: the newspaper fires him without cause and he doesn't put up a fight; someone drapes a coyote over his mail-box and he washes the dried blood off like it was bird droppings; Jessica rents a house in town and pays rent right out of the checkbook and he doesn't ask a single question. Sometimes it was all she could do to look at him without throwing something heavy.

She would be glad for the start of the new semester, glad for the end of summer, which had worn too long. She liked going into town every day, interacting with other people. Even though she would miss the long days of uninterrupted work on her sculpture, at least she wouldn't spend her days listening for the sound of Caleb's truck on the gravel or keep looking over her shoulder expecting to find him standing there, watch-ing her. No more of those awful long afternoons of silence, where he was always breaking into her brood to ask what was wrong, as if he didn't already know, as if he could do anything about it. The problem with Caleb was he thought he could fix anything if he just tinkered with it enough.

Over the last year or so, when things had gotten so bad, Caleb had backed off and given her the room she needed, even though they had never talked about it and Jessica had never said she needed the room. Caleb never asked about her teaching schedule, never questioned her leaving the house early in the morning or her coming home after supper, never complained about eating alone. He hadn't complained when she asked him to move the sculpture to school so she could work between classes. He'd just started figuring how to mount an A-frame to his tractor so he could winch it onto the flatbed. He didn't want to fight.

As she came into De Soto Jessica took the by-pass, missing the new Super WalMart, the mall, the

Pier One, the new home improvement center, and the string of franchised restaurants that had spread farther and farther out. She swung into the old part of town, just off downtown, into a neighborhood that had once thrived but had been left behind for blacks, Hispanics, Vietnamese, old white widows who refused to move out, and college students looking for cheap rent. Every third house seemed to be boarded over. She had signed another year's lease on the old house, again without telling Caleb. She was sure he knew. It was an old house with a sagging foundation, an air conditioner that never worked, and an arched door with stained glass panels where angels basked on the clouds. She looked forward to running a tub of hot water and slipping into it. During the school year she spent most mornings in the tub. She needed the time to wash off the smell of the woods, the smell of the wolves. She needed time to transform into that other person, the teacher who made assignments and critiqued and handed out grades to art students who believed they deserved an A for the attempt alone, regardless of how well their projects spoke. Jessica, who had never studied formally, the adjunct professor without a degree.

She had never felt comfortable at the university. Her credentials were nonexistent, her margins rough, and she felt as if the other faculty and students were always waiting for her to fall back into being a ship welder. There was nothing wrong with her technique, but the lines of her work felt too straight, too measured, her inspiration shallow. Deep down, she worried that the soaring eagle sculpture that had made such an impression on the art department had been a lucky find, and she worried what would happen when she unveiled "Natchez at Sunset." What would the

clucking tongues say once she had drifted off to another part of the reception and they crossed their arms
and cocked their heads and examined the sculpture
over their glasses of wine?

She tried not to think about it. She tried to trust
her tools and her eye. But the doubt was always there,
as was the suspicion, deep down, that what she did at
the university was not work. She had grown up working. Her father was a welder, and her mother cooked
at the Navy commissary. As a girl, Jessica's life had revolved around her parents' work—waking before dawn
to the smells of coffee and bacon and the tired groans
of her father and the patient weariness of her mother.
Evening conversations revolved around the politics of
working for defense contractors and military bases,
union business, tools, war, ship deployment. For Jessica, work meant being tired and dirty, but it had also
provided a solidarity that she missed now. Her mother
and father were friends with the people they worked
with. Her father fished, played cards, and watched
football with his buddies. Her mother had a group
of women friends from church, and when she wasn't
working she always seemed to be cooking for someone
who was sick, or preparing a Sunday school lesson. But
Jessica never felt comfortable in the Art department.
Everyone was polite, but the students whispered in
Art History and smiled at their private jokes—Jessica
was sure they made fun of her accent, the way she
struggled over French and Italian words—and to the
other professors, the ones with MFAs and PhDs, she
might as well have been the janitor. It was something
that Jessica missed—men and women friends, the solidarity of a workplace—something that Caleb couldn't
provide.

She had tried bringing Caleb to departmental functions. He invariably had a desperate look in his eye when he cast about for something to say about a painting or a sculpture. At parties he stood in the kitchen, a beer wrapped in his hand, and nodded a greeting whenever someone came within nodding distance. Jessica never had to ask if he was ready to leave. He didn't seem to need other people. He didn't fish, didn't drink in bars, and he didn't go to church anymore. Caleb liked to be at home or in the woods. He walked and swam with his wolves, drove gravel roads and listened to NPR on the radio, and he liked to be with Jessica. She smiled at that, but it bothered her too. Caleb seemed to need only her, and she felt guilty when she wasn't there.

Jessica pulled into her driveway and carried her bag inside and dropped it by the door. There was a pile of junk mail on the floor beneath the mail slot. She headed upstairs for the bathroom and the old claw-foot tub, shedding her clothes as she went. She opened the faucets and waited for the water to heat up, then added baby oil to the water and remembered sitting on the stool in her parents' bathroom, talking to her mother while she soaked away the bad parts of the day.

Jessica's foot flushed crimson as she tested the bath water. She eased in, feeling the warmth rise up her legs to her waist, spreading higher as she submersed. She held her breath under the water and opened her eyes. Her hair floated above her face. She and Caleb had tried everything. A year of planning their sex around her ovulations. Nights of him hovering over her, pumping away, workmanlike. The waiting, and the home pregnancy tests. Waiting for the next cycle, waiting without touching. Wearing out the Subaru driving to the clinic in Jackson. Caleb's surgery. He'd become expert at subcutaneous hormone injections intended to push her ovaries into producing healthy eggs. After four rounds of in vitro, eight thousand dollars a turn, even the doctors seemed to feel guilty about wasting their money. A second mortgage. Caleb was fired, and then he went all in on a used bull-dozer and a backhoe and earthmoving work, saying he'd never write another word. More in vitro. Working seven days a week, both of them. Waiting tables at night. Cutting logging roads into the national forest so the lumber companies could expand the clearcuts. Passing each other in brief moments. When they ac-cepted the fact that science couldn't help them, they had turned to adoption, only to find out that years of infertility treatments had left them too broke to pay legal fees. Finding Lacey. Losing Lacey. Losing Lacey's baby. Jessica stopped talking, and when she would answer Caleb's questions about what she was think-ing, she'd say "Alaska," just to have something to say. And then he came back from the equipment auction in Texas with another dozer and a pair of wolves. Two years of raising wolves—magical at times, but mostly frustrating. Almost a year since they'd had sex, last August, on the bank of the river. The sand held the sun's warmth even though it felt like emery cloth on her skin. Afterward, when they slipped into the river to rinse off, the silt-laden water flowed around her like a soft feather comforter. Wolves but no sex. And then the hate mail, the threats. Good ole boys don't like wolves in their deer woods, especially when they're out of work. Jessica sat up in the tub. She didn't know where to go from here.

Caleb worked the blade of the bulldozer into the side of the hill, shearing away the earth like shavings whittled from a block of wood, cutting new fire roads into the national forest. The big Cat responded to the touch of his hands and feet and the forest yielded, trees creaking and groaning and exploding with sharp cracks as the wood splintered and the trunks crashed to the ground, upper branches crashing through the surrounding canopy as they fell and leaves falling around him like the softest snowfall. Once the road was cut, he'd push the slash into windrows to burn. It was a good job, though sooner or later it would end. The Department of Agriculture was trying to clear cut every acre it could to starve Canada's pulp industry, and sooner than later there would be no need for fire roads to provide access to fire crews.

He ignored Hubert pulling up and parking behind him, safely out of the work zone. Hubert sat behind the wheel smoking a cigarette, probably thinking of some flaw to point out in Caleb's work. The forest was thick and the air stagnant and dust hung thick, clogging Caleb's respirator and caking the sweat running down his face. As the road opened up the breeze followed and the sunshine lit the interior of the forest for the first time since winter when the tree limbs had been bare.

Caleb shifted into reverse and pulled back on the clutches without looking behind him, guiding the Cat toward the hood of Hubert's pickup. The old man would tap his horn when Caleb got close enough to jangle his nerves. Caleb went two seconds beyond where he gauged Hubert's pickup should be, so far that he gritted his teeth waiting for the metal groan of the Dodge Ram buckling under his tracks, before he released the clutches and the Cat jerked to a stop. A cloud of dust washed over Caleb, and then, and only then, came the sound of the horn.

Caleb sighed and looked over his shoulder. The left track had missed the fender by six inches. Hubert sat in the driver's seat, his door open and his legs swung out to the side, rolling another cigarette. Caleb shut down the diesel and listened to it clank into silence, accompanied by scolding crows.

"You ought to blow that horn sometime. Let someone know you're behind them."

"God made your neck so it can twist." Hubert ran his tongue over the cigarette and smoothed out the seam. He offered it to Caleb, but he shook his head.

"You quit again?"

"Ten years ago."

Hubert stuck the cigarette between his lips and lit it. He stepped out of the truck and leaned against the rear fender. "Your idea or hers?"

Caleb leaned back in the Cat seat and propped his feet on the hood above the controls. The fresh cut earth smelled sour. A fox squirrel ran across a pine branch and leaped to another tree, chattering. Hubert exhaled and the smoke washed over Caleb before it dissipated into the trees.

"Reckon Indian River's going to leave a tree in the county for seed?"

"Don't look like it," Caleb said, stretching. The road he'd just cut didn't look too bad. There were a few spots he'd have to go back over so it wouldn't wash out in the first thunderstorm.

Ahead of him the orange ribbons disappeared into the forest. He turned back toward Hubert.

"You come out here to talk about pulpwood?"

Hubert looked up. His eyes were watery and blue. He picked a speck of tobacco off his tongue and looked away. "I went to the doctor."

"You don't believe in doctors."

Hubert cleared his throat and spat. "They found something on my lung. I've got to go back for more tests."

Caleb's stomach tightened. "What's that mean?"

"What do you think it means? I reckon I've got the cancer. I knew I would as soon as they started printing that warning on tobacco."

Caleb swung his legs off the hood of the Caterpillar and turned to face his father. "It doesn't have to mean that."

Hubert studied the tread tracks.

"What day you going?"

Hubert shrugged his shoulders and stepped out of the cab and walked down the new road a few steps. His ankles turned on the fresh churned soil. Hubert had never appeared fragile before.

"They going to get that timber out of this bottom, huh? It's about time." Hubert unzipped his fly. It took a long time to start.

"I guess so," Caleb said. His mother in the hospital. The waiting room. Women from church fussing over him while Hubert went in to see her.

"Well, I don't need a nurse just yet, and if I did I bet I can find one better looking than you."

"Forget it." Caleb turned back toward the operator's seat and put his hand on the ignition. "Is that all you come for?"

"I reckon," Hubert said. He walked back to his truck and climbed in.

"I'll see you, then. I've got a ways to cut today." Caleb cranked the bulldozer and adjusted the idle, then shifted into low and clanked toward the next stake. He didn't look around for a few minutes, but when he did, Hubert was gone.

The gravel road wound over the top of the hill and disappeared into the next bottom. The land on both sides of the road was an old clear cut forest coming back in waist high pines poking up behind the remnants of blackjack oak and beeches and gums the pulpwood mill couldn't use for paper. The hardwoods had been cut down and left to decompose, nutrients for the pine forest replacing them. The bark had dried and worn off the trunks, leaving them to go silver in the sun.

Near the top of the hill Caleb pulled over and shut off the pickup. He took a beer from the paper sack and opened it. Chain saws whined and a log skidder rumbled behind the next ridge, the sound carried on the light breeze. Jet contrails crisscrossed over wispy cirrus clouds against a blue sky. The sea of dark green marking the national forest had diminished into a perpetual low tide as the clearcut expanded, transitioning through progressively lighter shades from established saplings through yearlings to fresh-planted shoots in the harsh red soil of the most recent clearing. Columns of smoke rose from freshly torched windrows of trash trees and ash fell to the earth like the first large flakes of a snowfall. The deep green sea of pine rolling out of sight—broken by a lighter green line of bottomland hardwoods that marked the river and creeks running toward the Gulf of Mexico—was gone. It had only taken a couple of years. Fall, Caleb's favorite time of year when the heat broke and the hardwoods briefly flared into oranges, yellows and browns, felt like it would never come. And even when it did, it wouldn't be the same without the color. Winter, when the pines still retained their dark green and the hardwoods were reduced to silvery bare limbs feathering off into nothing, felt as far distant as the Second Coming of Christ.

A long time ago Caleb had had a poster framed and hung on the wall of his living room. He'd noticed it in college—an advertisement for a literary conference on Mississippi authors up at Ole Miss. One of his professors told him that the picture had been taken in South Mississippi sometime around the Civil War. It showed a man dressed in wool pants and old felt hat, sitting in front of a stand of long-leaf pines. The tree trunks were like nothing Caleb had ever seen. Thirty feet in circumference, so big it would take five tall men standing fingertip to fingertip to encircle the tree, the trunks rose beyond the scope of the picture, sixty feet without a branch. The forest floor was as clean as a park and the diamond-shaped slabs of bark as big as platters. The trees reminded Caleb of the pictures of redwoods in California—not big enough to drive a car through a tunnel cut in the trunk, but bigger than anything that had grown in Mississippi in over a hundred years.

The poster photo was credited to the archives of the forestry museum in Jackson, and Caleb had driven up there one Saturday. There were hardly any pictures to prove it, but the state forester told him that once all South Mississippi had looked like that. Single pines with enough board feet of lumber to build a house. Old growth cypress standing in swamps, surrounded by knobby knees that stood up out of the water like crenellations on a castle battlement. It was so long ago that nothing remained to prove their existence except for the antebellum mansions in Natchez and other small towns around the state. Even those massive stumps had long ago rotted. Caleb had sent off to Ole Miss for a copy of the poster. Thirty dollars.

Caleb had thought about going up to Ole Miss—as far as he could get from Hubert without paying out-of-state tuition, but he'd settled for Mississippi Southern in DeSoto, just up the road, borrowing money to pay for tuition and boarding because he knew it would piss Hubert off even more. He'd delivered sandwiches for Po-Boy Express, practiced journalism on campus events, and copy-edited at the *Three Rivers Daily*, taking the job after graduation without ever leaving the county. At times he thought he'd missed a big opportunity, especially when he thought about Jessica in Alaska, but he'd never wanted to get too far away from the land, which seemed wild enough. Once he got out of school he been surprised when Hubert deeded him a chunk of land that made them neighbors, and he'd looked at that as his father's tacit apology for his childhood following his mother's death.

Caleb often thought about that day when he was twelve years old and riding the fields on his three-wheeler, checking on the cattle, which was his chore every day after school. The cow was already down on its side when he found it, its neck twisted up to the sky and bellowing in pain and fear. The other cattle had scattered across the field and resumed grazing. They weren't even curious, and Caleb wondered why they didn't at least stand closer to intimidate the coyotes which were sure to come running with the smell of blood and afterbirth.

Caleb hopped off the three-wheeler and slowly approached. The cow's eyes were rolled up in its head so the whites were showing, and its tongue—stuck out to one side—was coated with dirt, grass, and phlegm. He knelt and touched the cow's belly, but it rolled onto its back and kicked. A hoof caught Caleb in the side and sent him sprawling. He lay in a pile of fresh cowshit, gasping for breath, wondering how many ribs had been broken. The cow struggled to its feet and trotted a few feet away, trailing blood, but then it began to sway back and forth. The cow's side undulated as it struggled to give birth. One hoof extended from between the cow's legs, turned so that Caleb could see the calf was breeched. Caleb stared at the cow's sides rippling, fascinated, though he had seen it plenty of times.

He had seen his father reach inside a cow and turn the calf; he'd seen him grab two legs and yank the calf out, but he didn't think there was time to ride back for Hubert. If the cow lay down again it wouldn't stand up, and if that happened it would die. Caleb rolled to his hands and knees and felt the nausea wash over him. He threw up, and then struggled to his feet tasting acid. He walked toward the cow, holding his hands out to calm it, but the animal looked at him wild-eyed and ran away each time. Caleb made clucking noises and spoke softly, but the cow wouldn't settle. They moved across the field that way, the other cattle shifting to give them room, only looking up in mild curiosity for a moment before returning to their graze. Once, Caleb got close enough to get a hand on the hoof. The smell was overpowering and it made him gag, but he set his feet and yanked as hard as he could. His hands slipped. He fell backward, igniting the pain in his ribs. He lay in the dirt and cried until the pain ebbed away while the cow staggered across the field and settled to the ground with a loud groan. It lay there, breathing heavily. Caleb lay a few feet away, watching, afraid to go home and tell his father. He planned his lie, how the cow had kicked him and knocked him unconscious. He didn't think Hubert could blame him for that.

Just before dark Hubert parked his pickup twenty feet away and walked over to where Caleb was standing, staring down at the cow.

Hubert looked at the cow and waited. Caleb didn't say anything.

"Don't you know it's suppertime?"

"I tried to help it, but I couldn't get it to stand still long enough. It just kept running away from me."

Hubert shook his head and muttered to himself. He took off his straw hat and wiped his forehead with his sleeve, then swung his arm and slapped Caleb with the hat. He stumbled backward and fell. Hubert bent over him and slapped him over the head and shoulders with the hat, scratching his face and bloodying his lip.

"Why didn't you come get me?"

"There wasn't time."

"So you just let it lay down?"

"I tried to turn it the way I seen you do. It wouldn't stop running."

Hubert walked off, talking to himself. Caleb stood up, shaking, and dusted himself off. It hurt to breathe. Hubert turned and stalked back.

"That's a thousand dollars' worth of cow you let die, cow and calf." He raised his hat again and Caleb turned away to cover himself, wincing at the pain in his side.

"Quit crying. You ain't hurt yet."

"I got kicked."

Hubert ran his hands over Caleb's ribs.

His touch felt almost tender.

"I guess we should go to the doctor."

"I don't know that I can ride my three-wheeler."

"You rode it out here, you can ride it home."

Caleb nodded, said "yessir," and limped over to the three-wheeler. Pulling the starter cord nearly made him pass out, but one look over his shoulder at Hubert made him straighten and give the cord a second yank. The man stood there like a dog bred to fight, looking for a weakness. Riding home, with every stab of pain, Caleb wished Hubert an eternity of hellfire.

The beer in the sack had grown warm, so Caleb reached for the ignition. And now Hubert had cancer. The old man had never asked for help or sympathy, never given any. That's fine, Caleb thought. He shifted into gear and started home.

Jessica moved across the scaffold, swabbing the copper sheet clouds with a chromium arsenate solution. The glow of the sunset tempered the light inside the Quonset hut, helping the sculpture glow in a weak imitation of the outside violets and blues and reds and oranges that she could not seem to capture. Green and gold fireflies drifted through the trees. Behind her the radio crackled with static. She looked at Caleb. He turned the volume down, but not off.

Jessica couldn't see the point of listening to a game on the radio. She appreciated the commentary on the weather, the images of families out for an evening, and the idle chatter about the ballpark food, but she had difficulty trying to follow the action on the field: the placement of runners, the trajectory of the ball and the reactions of the fielders. Brief moments of confusion to interrupt the endless description of balls and strikes and fouls. Listening to football was only slightly better, but at least she could gauge the success of a play based on the down and distance.

This Texas Rangers business was something new for Caleb. For their first ten years together, she hadn't known baseball existed, and then suddenly, he's scrolling the AM dial, explaining about getting better reception after the sun goes down. Apparently, radio waves traveled longer distances at night. He was acting different that afternoon. He'd fiddled around the hut, making work out of nothing, like he wanted to talk about something but couldn't decide how.

She lit the acetylene torch and adjusted the flame, then passed it over the copper sheets, experimenting with the temperature and duration to see how the chemicals changed the metal. Acetylene soot drifted up from the flame and adhered to the sculpture's clouds, so that the dark spots looked like the V-shape of flying birds. She wondered how to make the birds more permanent. The buildings of Natchez nestled into the hill and the Mississippi flowed past, rushing toward New Orleans.

It wasn't working. Not in this light. Not on this day. Jessica closed the valve on her torch and placed it on the platform, then pulled off her goggles and stared at her sculpture, making a point of ignoring Caleb, who had found a greasy cardboard box of parts to go through.

Jessica pulled off her work shirt and wiped the sweat off her face with the tail. She plucked at the tank top she wore underneath, trying to cool down. She felt Caleb's eyes on her, but he looked back to his parts.

"How's it looking?" he asked.

She shook her head, studied the sculpture. "Like shit."

He looked at the sculpture and back at her. He seemed lost for words, so she softened. "What's this sudden interest in baseball?"

"Oh," Caleb said, relieved. "My dad used to listen to baseball at night. We could get Dallas after dark, and sometimes we'd just sit out in the pasture at night, listening to the game."

"You have a pleasant memory of your childhood?" She smiled. "I don't know what to think."

"I heard Texas might make the playoffs. I bet he figures that's a sure sign the world is going to hell."

"I'm sure he's heard that on the radio. I think I even heard it on NPR."

"It feels like it, sometimes." Caleb said.

Jessica frowned, wiping at her face with the tail of her tank top. She wondered how much soot she was wearing and how badly it had smeared.

Caleb dropped a hydraulic coupling into the box and wiped his hands on his jeans. "So what's not working with the piece?" he asked. "It looks fine to me."

"Fine?"

"Yeah, fine." He stared at the sculpture the way he used to stare at the computer screen when he was writing a tough piece. "I mean, I can see what you're trying to do with it, anyway."

"Say something about it. Something critical."

A long pause. Jessica noticed the cicada hum, realized they had raised their voices just to talk over the insect roar.

"I don't know." He looked like a college student who hadn't done his homework.

"You're a word man," she said. "At least you used to be." It always surprised her when he did feel moved to talk. He could stake the wolves out on their chains and sit for hours and watch them work a pasture for mice, occasionally commenting on the beauty of their stiff legged pounces that stunned the mice and made them easy to catch. He could talk about the sunset, about the moon on clouds and the shadows they cast on the earth, about the shifting center of the V formation geese used in migration. How hard could it be to say something about her sculpture?

"I don't know," Caleb said. "I'm not an art critic."

Jessica parted her lips, feeling the promise of hope for the evening slipping away. She climbed off the scaffold and closed the main valve on her acetylene tank, gave him a long look.

"Want to go down to the river?" Caleb asked.

She shook her head. "Not tonight. I think I might get cleaned up and go into town. Get a milkshake or something."

Caleb nodded. "I don't mind going with you."

"No," she said. "You listen to your game. I'll be okay."

She pulled her goggles over her head and hung them on the valve of the tank by their strap. She walked past Caleb, but stopped at the entrance to the Quonset hut and pulled the bandana out of her hair. "You know I've got a place in town, right?"

"Yeah."

"I haven't tried to hide it, or anything. I write the checks every month and enter them."

"I've seen it," Caleb said.

Jessica took a deep breath. "This isn't going to sound good any way I say it." She looked away and ran the back of a hand over her cheek. "I think I want to stay there for a while."

Caleb stared at her. She couldn't tell if he was angry, hurt, or just didn't care. She turned and started for the house.

The ballgame came in and out as the dark fell. Mosquitos, cicadas, and tree frogs grew out of the night and overwhelmed the commentary on the radio. The commercials between innings sounded tinny and repetitive and didn't touch any part of Caleb's life any more than the traffic in Dallas affected his mornings. He didn't know any of the names of the players anymore and the game crept along. He wondered what Jessica was doing.

He grabbed a flashlight and followed the white circle, watching for snakes. A few small animals scuttled away from the trail, and far away he could hear a whip-poor-will calling over and over. He wasn't in the mood to wrestle the wolves into their harnesses, but they regressed if they missed even one night of handling. Not having Jessica made it worse.

The wolves were in a mood; Max knocked Caleb down a couple of times and then when he got them harnessed, they pulled him along the trail like a sled. He dug in a couple of times and tried to jerk the animals off their feet, like training a dog to heel, but they barely slowed and he gave up and let them pull him along. He turned off the flashlight and stuck it in his back pocket, knowing the wolves would drive away the rattlesnakes. The water was low and the sand and gravel bar stretched around the curve of the river, the beach shining bright in the weak moonlight against the dark woods and water.

Caleb tied off the wolves to their logging chains and let them go. He walked downstream, letting his eyes attune to the dark. At the edge of the water a compact coil flopped and swam away, rippling the water in silver rings. His stomach turned on seeing the water moccasin and he moved back from the water. It was hard not to imagine a snake under every rock once he had seen one.

He sat down and brushed away a persistent mosquito and watched the wolves wade the river, trying to not think about Jessica. In the early days they walked every evening and usually ended up on this sandbar. If the weather was warm, it was likely they would take their clothes off and, Jessica leading him into the water, slide into the smooth coolness and wrap themselves together. Later, they would spread a blanket or a sleeping bag onto the sand, and after, they would lay together, her head on his stomach, and look at the sky and talk about almost anything. He had been happy. Until the infertility, he thought she had been happy.

After a couple of years together they had begun to talk about having children, Jessica feeling the urgency more than Caleb, who—given Hubert as a model— worried about what sort of father he might make. Still, there was the belief that he could do better, and knowing how much it meant to Jessica, he had begun to imagine the possibilities. They made love on a schedule, dutifully following Jessica's ovulation pattern, abstaining for a few days before each cycle began, measuring her temperature and keeping charts of her periods, buying pregnancy tests, only to be disappointed month after month. Jessica kept a pile of books beside her bed, everything known about the science of getting pregnant, including the *Kama Sutra*.

Sex without spontaneity became another chore. After a year Jessica wanted to get help, so she scheduled an appointment with an infertility clinic. Caleb thought it too soon. The idea of doctors prodding his wife, asking questions about their private lives and habits, turned him cold. In the six weeks before the appointment, Caleb lost interest in sex. Jessica continued to track her ovulations, but when she asked him to come to bed, Caleb said, "We've got the appointment now. Let's wait and see what the doctor says."

Jessica had pulled away from him. Caleb knew it was the wrong move, but he hadn't been able to get past it.

The truth was, Caleb knew, that he had been ready to support Jessica's infertility. She had worried so much about her past—some pot in the 80s, mushrooms, the long-term effects of breathing welding fumes and living in the electromagnetic field of a high voltage arc welder her adult life—that Caleb had just assumed she was infertile. In the parking lot outside the clinic he'd patted her leg and said, "No matter what they tell us, I love you and I'll always love you and we'll do whatever it takes."

They were seen in a plain office by a woman, a short, abrupt doctor who spoke, it seemed to Caleb, only to Jessica. She asked question after question about Jessica's health and sex history. Jessica guided her through the regularity of her periods and the methods of birth control. She blushed her way through her sex partners, not naming names but counting to six before coming to Caleb. There had been two miscarriages. Her intercourse history started at eighteen, Caleb noted, meaning sometime in Alaska. A little of it Caleb had known, but neither of them had ever pushed for details about each other's sex lives. He studied a poster on sexually transmitted diseases and was caught up short when asked about his own history.

Caleb was embarrassed that his list was shorter. He had never gotten a girl pregnant, to his knowledge, though there had been a long week waiting for a period, once. He evaded the doctor's question about masturbation, and mumbled "once in a while."

She pressed him and he answered truthfully.

"Thank you," she'd said, making notes on her legal pad. "Now, can you describe the volume and viscosity of the ejaculate?"

Caleb took a deep breath and let it out. "I don't pay that much attention."

The doctor pressed further, making the question a multiple choice rather than a fill in the blank, and Caleb chose as best he could. She nodded and flipped her legal pad to a fresh page and began to sketch what turned out to be the female reproductive system and began a lecture on getting pregnant, like Caleb and Jessica were teenagers in sex-ed. The way the doctor explained it, though, in terms of pure odds—what was supposed to happen and what often prevented it from happening—pregnancy was much more of a miracle than Caleb had been led to believe. The doctor closed by describing possible procedures and costs for a variety of solutions ranging from adoption to donor sperm to in vitro fertilization.

"A test tube baby?" Caleb asked.

"That's archaic terminology," the doctor said. Then she smiled at Jessica and leaned forward. "What are you thinking?"

Jessica looked at Caleb, her eyes a question. "I don't know where to start," she said.

"Why don't we do a physical exam, then," the doctor said. "Mr. Vogel, you can stay for this if Mrs. Vogel is okay with it."

Caleb didn't say anything, but Jessica nodded.

"Mrs. Vogel," the doctor continued. "This is a long process—I'm talking months—to find answers for a couple's infertility. It's almost never easy, and the odds aren't always good. There will be plenty of time for questions as we go along."

Jessica nodded, a bit too eagerly, Caleb thought.

A nurse led them into an exam room. In one corner was a bed with stainless steel extensions at the foot and a counter with sink and cabinets. She gave Jessica a gown and told her the doctor would be back in a few minutes, then closed a curtain over their corner of the room.

Jessica looked at the gown, finding the front and ties. "Staying?" she asked.

"Sure."

"Up to you."

Caleb turned to the counter and tried a couple of drawers, embarrassed to watch Jessica undress in an exam room.

When the doctor came in she told Jessica to place her feet in the stirrups. During the examination Jessica stared at Caleb's face. The doctor warned her when a touch might hurt, and as she worked under Jessica's spread gown, Jessica would wince and draw her breath. She looked more scared than in pain.

Caleb watched, not sure what to think, but he pulled in close to the screen while the doctor used ultrasound to examine Jessica's uterus and count the follicles on her ovaries. The screen was an alien landscape.

When she finished the doctor seemed pleased. There didn't seem to be any structural abnormalities, she said, although there was still some blood work and other tests to determine hormonal levels. She gave Jessica a smile and a pat of encouragement. "We're already ruling out some possible causes," she said. "You can get dressed now, Mrs. Vogel, but there's one more thing we need to do today." She turned to Caleb. "Have you ejaculated in the past forty-eight hours Mr. Vogel?"

He looked at her.

"Would you be opposed to providing us with a semen specimen today?"

"I guess not," he said. The doctor wasn't smiling, but to Caleb she was laughing her ass off behind those straight lips. His face flushed. Jessica was trying not to smile. He leaned against the counter and studied the laminate pattern of the countertop, listening to the doctor give orders to a nurse. She left the room and the doctor pointed Caleb toward the hallway, where he was supposed to wait.

The nurse was pretty, mid-twenties, and somehow more professional than Caleb could stand. She came down the hallway with a clipboard clapped to her chest. Caleb tried not to make eye contact. He wished she had been sixty and mean tempered.

"Ready Mr. Vogel?"

He nodded and followed her to a room off the hallway. The walls were institutional tan, like the other rooms in the unit, but otherwise the room was made up to look like a little motel room: A small bed with a pillow and a nightstand beside it, a vinyl couch against the wall, and an empty laundry hamper. Clean sheets were folded and lay on one end of the couch.

The covers on the bed were turned back enough to see a sheet and hospital blanket under a thin floral pattern bedspread. There was a sink and a paper towel dispenser above it.

The nurse closed the door and gave Caleb a reassuring smile. "Once I leave you'll have complete privacy," she said. "The door can't be opened from the outside and you can take as long as you need. Feel free to make out the couch or you can use the bed. There's reading material in the nightstand. Questions?" He shook his head. She walked over to a small door in the wall and pulled it open. Inside was a specimen cup, which she handed to Caleb. "Just make sure that you collect the entire specimen in the cup," she said, "and when you're finished you can put the cup back in here"—she opened the door as if there was some trick to it—"and just flip this switch." She pointed to a light switch beside the door. "When you're finished you can get dressed and leave. You don't have to check out with anyone. Questions?"

Caleb said no, and she headed for the door.

"Good luck," she said.

After she left, Caleb checked the door to make sure it was locked. It still opened from his side, but when he tried the outside handle it wouldn't turn, so he closed it. He looked around the room, pushed on the bed, but couldn't bring himself to sit down on it. The texture of the cover reminded him of cheap hotel rooms from spring break trips to Biloxi and New Orleans. He opened the nightstand drawer and saw a stack of *Playboy* and *Penthouse* magazines, the covers worn. The date on the top magazine was a couple of years old. He unfolded a sheet onto the couch and thumbed through the *Playboy*.

The magazine hadn't changed since college, still the girl next door look. The *Penthouses* were raunchier, with girls having sex with both men and women. The girls in the magazine were pretty enough, but heavy breasted, and what lingerie they wore—too many feathers and too much lace. He pulled a few more magazines out of the drawer without looking beyond the cover, but then he was surprised to find some photos printed out on copier paper. Caleb sorted through a handful of pages. The pictures looked like they came off the internet, not much different than the *Penthouse* pictures. Caleb wondered if part of the nurse's job was to find "reading material," or if guys just brought their own. He stopped at a picture printed from a private photo. Not a model. No airbrushing. The girl was pretty, beautiful even, and clean cut in a way that the girls in *Playboy* couldn't be. This girl had been shot on a patio somewhere, printed in black and white. She lay on her back on a picnic table, her head in the foreground, hanging slightly off the end of the table and smiling at the photographer as if he was someone she liked. Her breasts were modestly covered with one forearm. Her other hand gripped the pole of the table's umbrella, and her feet were planted on the table and her knees in the air. A low brick wall and shrubbery formed the backdrop.

Caleb stared at the picture, wondering who would bring a picture into a room, use it, and then leave it for the next guy. He felt the start of an erection and decided it was time to get started, but then he wondered how much time it should take. He imagined the people in the lab on the other side of the room, waiting for the light to flash so they could open the door in the wall and remove the sample. He wondered if they made bets on how long it would take. Five minutes seemed

too efficient and businesslike for something so complicated as making a baby, and thirty minutes would
make it look like he either had a problem, or he was
enjoying himself too much in the little room with the
couch and bed and the pornography. He wondered if
guys undressed and got in the bed and covered themselves. He couldn't imagine taking the time to do that.
He wondered if they laid out multiple magazines, or
even how choosy they were over the pictures. He wondered if just the picture was enough for most guys, or
if they had to make up a story about the girl as well. He
tried not to think about what other men had done with
the picture. Thinking wasn't helping anything, and he
could feel the erection slipping away. He needed to get
finished and get out.

He unbuckled his belt and slid his pants down.
He realized he didn't want to use the patio girl that
way, and he put her back in the drawer and picked up
the first *Playboy,* found a picture and started to work,
holding the specimen cup in one hand. It didn't take
long, and when he finished, he set the cup aside and
waddled over to the sink, washed his hands, dried them
with a paper towel, and then pulled his jeans back up
and fastened them.

After he put the specimen in the wall and flipped
the switch, he looked at the room. He gathered the
magazines and put them back in the drawer and shut
it, but then he pulled out the picture of the patio girl.
He looked at her for a few seconds, then folded the
picture twice and stuck it in his back pocket. The hallway was clear when he opened the door and he headed
down the hall, intent on getting back to the pickup. He
figured Jessica would find him there sooner or later. He
looked both ways and seeing no one, pushed the girl's

picture into a trash can and tried not to think about it anymore.

Two days later the doctor called with the results of the semen analysis: low sperm count and low motility in the few sperm he did have. The odds of conceiving by intercourse were astronomical. The doctor recommended Caleb schedule an exam with a urologist to try and discover what might be causing his problem. Otherwise, the only option was in vitro fertilization, an expensive long shot. Caleb tried to put a brave face on the news. He joked about shooting blanks, and Jessica appeared sympathetic. But looking back at it now, and watching the wolves wade across the creek to the end of their logging chains, Caleb knew that a lot of what happened to him and Jessica next—their sex life dwindling to nothing, Jessica picking up the second apartment in town, the wolves—was mostly his fault. Finding out that he was infertile hit him in a way that he couldn't have predicted. Deep down. Maybe even a message from the God he had given up on a long time ago. Maybe he didn't need to be a father, no more than Hubert needed to be a father. It kept him up at night.

Caleb went along with everything Jessica wanted, despite believing that they were doomed to failure. The next few months were marked by countless trips to the urologist, more visits to the specimen room to masturbate, semen analyses that never changed, and eventually surgery. They tried multiple cycles of in vitro fertilization; Caleb began to pick up earthmoving work to help pay for it, after he'd posted his articles for the day. Jessica submitted to the month of nightly injections the nurse taught Caleb to give, which built up to the implantation of the fertilized embryo, and they waited through the two weeks after the procedure for the scheduled pregnancy test, only to be disappointed. Then they waited until another cycle could begin. The hormone shots twisted Jessica's moods like an ant trail, and Caleb pulled away from her with each failed cycle. But each new cycle he gamely came up with the extra money to pay for another round. Disappointed over and over again. Finally, even the doctor was reluctant to try any more.

The mosquito wouldn't go away, no matter how often Caleb brushed at it. It alternated between ears, zooming in with a maddening high-pitched drone. The wolves made light splashes in the water as they snapped at floating leaves or things that Caleb couldn't see in the dark. He thought about fall weather and wished it would hurry. He thought of brisk air and bright colors, snakes retreating into their holes and mosquitos dying off, football season. There were mixed blessings as well. The start of school for Jessica would take her away from him more often—he suspected that if she moved into town she would only come out on weekends—but she was happier when she was busy. Long summer days gave her too much time. With the start of hunting season, whoever was sending him letters, whoever was decorating his mailbox, would have something to keep him busy. More people with guns in the woods, and the possibility of Max and Lulu being mistaken for coyotes. He wondered how Hubert would respond to his treatments, but he couldn't imagine any scenario with his father that would turn out good.

The mosquito settled in for a bite and Caleb squashed it with a slap. He enjoyed the satisfaction of smearing his own blood across the back of his neck. He stood up and walked over to the logging chains, bent down and gave Lulu a tug. It was never easy getting the wolves started back to the pen, but sometimes if he could get Lulu started, Max was more likely to follow along.

Hubert squinted against the smoke of his cigarette and unrolled the newspaper. The president was in trouble about his Twitter again, whatever the hell that was. He was picking fights with just about everyone: word fights and trade wars with England, Germany, Brazil, and Canada. He really had it in for China. Real fights with pretty much all of the Holy Land. Muslims were killing Muslims in the desert and Christians and homosexuals in Europe, and the president was shooting missiles into Iran and Syria. There was another school shooting in Kentucky and more liberals wanting to take away guns, but the president was having none of that. Russia was moving tanks into countries Hubert had thought were already Russia, countries he hadn't heard of since Reagan. A black church had been burned in Tupelo and a mosque had been blown up in Los Angeles. The camel-jockeys that had been in the country when the president took over were packed off to prison or sent home. Business at Guantanamo Bay was booming. The Mexicans were coming over the border in droves and getting caught, and the bleeding hearts were crying about wetback children separated from their parents and locked in cages. Kansas, Nebraska, and Colorado were caught in a two-year long drought and prairie fires were sweeping toward the airport in Denver, grounding flights. The Mississippi had caught fire below St. Louis. There was another protest march in Washington, but Hubert didn't bother to see who it was this time.

He figured about half the news was made up, anyway, and the rest he approved of. He didn't have it
in for the blacks and the Mexicans, but he had never
been able to get past Viet Nam or what the Japs had
done to the country at Pearl Harbor, and as far as the
Muslim rag-head terrorists went, he figured any oil
they were setting on was owed to the US for 9/11, and
the Muslim president should have taken it instead of
giving it all back to them.

He kept skimming, growing more and more angry,
until he got to the front page of the local section.
The headline read "Another Cow Mutilation Baffles
Authorities." The picture was supposed to be a cow's
head, but it reminded him of a county fair exhibition
he'd paid twenty-five cents to see when he was a boy,
a sorry mess that was supposed to be an alien baby.
This latest mutilation had been found in Oktibbeha
County, and it featured an interview with an animal
husbandry professor from Mississippi State. The bull
had been found by a rancher who'd called in the sheriff, who then called in the professor. He read:

The bull was lying on its left side in a muddy
pasture. Its right ear and eye were missing, cut
clean from the animal's head. In the ear's place
was a tiny teardrop pattern, no blood. The eye
socket was surrounded by a clean circle where
the flesh had been neatly removed to the bone.
Again, no blood.

And below, the flesh from the right side
of the jaw had been excised with surgical pre-
cision. As well, the tongue was missing, re-
moved from deep within the bull's throat. The
animal's scrotum was gone and its anus com-
pletely cored out.

An autopsy couldn't reveal how the bull was actually killed, and according to the sheriff there were no animal tracks, or any evidence of crows or buzzards feeding on the carcass. There were fresh coyote tracks within thirty feet, but apparently the animal hadn't come any closer. And there were no human footprints whatsoever. It had come a heavy rain two days before the bull was found.

The rancher was quoted as saying "there's no common sense explanation for what happened here last night. You tell me how any animal or human is going to wrestle a 2,000 pound bull to the ground and skin it so clean without drawing blood and without leaving footprints? I don't think it's cults. There ain't any gum wrappers, no cigarette butts, and they don't leave any of their instruments."

The article said this was the second recorded mutilation in Oktibbeha County, and one of the dozen or so reported throughout the rest of the state. Similar cases had been reported in Alabama, Louisiana, Arkansas, and Tennessee.

Besides the university professor, the article interviewed another specialist on animal mutilations, who believed that the responsible party was some form of alien intelligence. When he got to the part about glowing lights, beams, discs, and alien encounters, Hubert put the paper away. It sounded like some of the nonsense Caleb used to write about.

"Lord, have mercy," he said. He ground out his cigarette and dropped the butt in the jar, picked up his thermos of coffee, and went out to check on his cattle. The shotgun was cradled in the rear window gun rack, loaded, just like always.

Jessica rented a truck to take her sculpture into town, then she packed her bags. Caleb sat on the porch, sipping coffee and watching her load her things into the Subaru, feeling like it might be more final than she would admit. When she came out with only two bags he was surprised. But later, when he looked inside her closet upstairs, he realized that her things must have been steadily working their way to her house in town over the last year. A change of clothes and a laptop computer one weekend, a small appliance or some pots and pans the next, the guest bed and a couple of chairs the next. Jessica had moved out without his noticing.

"Is that everything?" he asked. She had set the two bags on the porch and sat beside him to finish her coffee.

"It's what I need for right now. I left a few things that I can come back for. I've still got some equipment and material in the shop."

"It's going to be lonely."

"It's not forever." Jessica brushed a strand of hair out of her eyes.

"Do you want to walk down and see them before you go?"

"I don't need to make myself feel worse than I already do."

"I still don't understand," Caleb said.

"I don't either," Jessica said. She reached for his hand and squeezed it.

"Maybe—"

Jessica sighed and stood up. "I'm going now." She started to walk away, but she paused and turned back. "Hey, I left you a present under your pillow. Take it as a good sign."

She kissed Caleb on the cheek, then climbed into the car and took her sunglasses down from the visor, tossed a little wave, and drove away.

Caleb stood on the porch until the crunch of tires on gravel faded. It was a warm day, but a cool front had brought a storm overnight and had driven the clouds from the sky.

He walked inside and rinsed out his coffee cup and put it on the drain board to dry. He wandered upstairs and stood beside the bed for a long time, staring at his pillow. He pulled the spread back and lifted the pillow. It was a silver ring worked with Celtic runes, the type of piece he hadn't seen her make in years. It lay on a folded blue slip that she liked to sleep in some nights. He picked up the ring and turned it over, reading the symbols, and wondered if they really meant anything or if she'd just picked them out of a book. The slip still smelled like her. He held it a moment, then placed it back on the bed. He slipped the ring over his finger and it fit, but he took it off and placed it back on the slip and covered them with the pillow, then got ready for work.

During the night they talked on the phone. She said she missed him. She said she might come out and see the wolves that weekend, but she wasn't sure. A short silence, and then he told her that he wanted to make whatever they had work out, but she had said, "we'll see," and then laughed.

She said, "Kids always hate it when an adult says 'we'll see,' because it usually means no."

"Is that what it means now?"

"I don't know what it means," she said.

Caleb left it like that. "I'm taking my dad into the hospital in the morning. He's starting chemotherapy."

After long enough for Caleb to think the call had been dropped, she said, "That's tough."

"I just thought I'd let you know I'll be in town. Maybe I could stop by and have a cup of coffee while I'm waiting."

"I've got the sculpture. The show's coming."

"That's right."

"You should focus on your father. He'll need a lot of attention."

"He won't take help," Caleb said. "You know that."

"He should be thankful for what he gets."

Caleb nodded at the phone, then said: "I'm not sure what to do with all of this."

"Your father?"

"Him, you, everything."

"You've got to find one thing to focus on," Jessica said. "And right now it ought to be your father. That's the least thing you have control over."

"I don't have control over anything."

"It just feels that way," Jessica said. "What you have to watch out for is how your father is going to change. The medicines eat away your inside. He'll age right before your eyes."

"Is that what happened to your mother?" It was something Jessica would never talk about, her mother's cancer, her death, although it had been six years now. Caleb had tried to go with Jessica down to the coast to be with her mother the last few days, but she had kept him here. When he'd asked why she said she didn't know, but that it felt right.

"Yes. It happened to my mother. It happened to your mother. Don't you remember?"

Caleb did remember it, though as the years went on he found it harder. "It seems strange doesn't it?"

"What?"

"The way cancer creeps through our lives. It's like we're being stalked. My mother. Your mother. Now my dad."

"I'd go crazy if I thought that way," Jessica said, her voice distant. Not annoyed, like it had been when she answered the phone. She sounded like she hadn't slept in a week.

"So, what do I do?"

There were strange background noises on the phone. He wondered if she had walked off without hanging up, the way she sometimes did to telemarketers, allowing them to rattle out their sales pitch until they figured out no one was listening. It occurred to him that she might not be sure exactly what he was asking, and really, he didn't know himself. But then he heard her throat clear. "What you've got to do is find a picture of him, an old picture that will remind you of the way he used to look. The way you want to remember him. Keep it with you all the time."

"He never sat still for pictures."

"I can't help you with that." She sounded sorry.

"I'll find something."

They talked for a minute or two, and then hung up. Caleb stared at the phone for a long time, wishing it would ring.

He picked up the shotgun he'd started carrying since she'd left. He hadn't told her about the second coyote, shot and laid across the driveway with a ribbon tied around its neck. Phone calls with no one there when he answered. Pickups on the road flying Rebel flags, slowing in front of the house. Cigarette butts and beer cans in the woods—not too close to the wolf pens— but where people hadn't been by accident. On Caleb's property. The wind had shifted and there was always the smell of smoke from the clear-cut fires, up-setting Max and Lulu. He started for the wolf pen, but stopped before he got to the door. Too tired to move, too tired to make any effort, he wanted to go to sleep, but he knew it was too early and he would only toss and turn.

After Jessica hung up she tightened her robe and tied off the waist. She had been in a good mood until he called, just sitting on the couch, not doing anything, enjoying total relaxation. There was no one to talk to and nothing that needed to be said. Her clothes trailed across the floor of the living room where she had dropped them when she came home from work and slipped into her robe. The dishes from supper were stacked in the sink. They would get done when she needed clean ones, just as her clothes would be washed when she needed more. It felt good not to stand up from the table and walk to the sink and begin washing, as she had to do to beat Caleb to it, since he had been trained by his father to never rest while a chore was unfinished. It felt good to lose her keys and rings and purse somewhere in the house, wherever she happened to drop them, knowing that a short search would turn them up, and not have to worry about Caleb's impatience when she made him wait on her to leave the house. Caleb's things were always in the same place: his wallet in his hip pocket, his keys and change in his left front pocket, his knife and watch in his right pocket. He didn't empty his pockets to sit around the house, or even take off his jeans until he was ready to swim, shower, make love, or go to sleep. Occasionally, when Jessica couldn't find her key ring, he refused to loan her the keys they had in common. If he did, he snatched his keys out of her ignition as soon as she turned the motor off and stuffed them back into his pocket.

She almost hadn't answered the phone when it rang, knowing it would be him. But after twelve rings she had given in. She sounded angrier than she'd intended. His confusion was obvious, and for a moment she felt sorry for him. But she put him off about the weekend, even though she wanted to see Max and Lulu. When he started talking about his father she could feel herself pulling back, even though she tried to stop it. She could feel herself tucking into a tiny ball, like when she was a little girl and crawled behind the couch for no other reason than because she was tiny enough to fit there and because it felt so safe.The six years since her mother's death had done little t o ease her loss. It did feel like something was stalking her, and no matter how much she tried to forget it, it was always there. Her mother's cancer had crept up on her. She had gone in for a checkup one day and walked out knowing that she had cancer. Five weeks later she was dead.

Almost everyone she knew had a connection to someone with cancer. The woman news anchor on channel nine pushed self-exams on the ninth of the month, and Caleb almost always bought the breast cancer awareness stamps from the post office, as if he thought he was doing something useful. Jessica refused to examine herself, and she had never had a mammogram, although her doctor fussed at her whenever she had the chance. She had stopped having sex with Caleb partly out of fear of what she might feel as he cupped her breasts.

Sometimes Jessica found herself thinking that it was truly merciful that her mother had died so fast. There had been little talk of treatment. Mainly, her doctor was interested in pain control. She hadn't lingered, and Jessica had supposed that she would die under the medication haze. But the last couple of days her mother refused to take the medicine. She wanted to be lucid for the time she had left.

Jessica had seen a movie once where a woman did that to her son. Made him sit with her while she was dying and refusing to take her medicines. The movie had portrayed the act as a heroic effort, as a last chance for mother and son to establish some sort of bond. The two talked about everything, and the mother compared the pain of death to the pain of childbirth. She said philosophical things along the lines of, "without pain there cannot be life, and death, like life, is beautiful too." At least that's the way Jessica remembered the movie. Her mother's death had not been inspirational or beautiful. It had been gruesome and horrifying—short but gruesome. It made Jessica want to crawl behind the couch again.

The last night of her life, she told Jessica that she didn't want to die in the night with the creatures she hallucinated. Her pulse jumped and her heart muscles weren't firing properly. She had trouble getting enough oxygen, and she was working so hard to breathe that Jessica could feel the heat radiating off her body like a cooling oven. The hospital room was freezing, but it wasn't cold enough to ease her mother, so a nurse brought in a box fan and sat it at the foot of her bed. Jessica huddled under a blanket and watched her mother's heart monitor. A cuff took her blood pressure every fifteen minutes. The numbers were low, but they rose toward morning. Jessica thought about colored light, a prayer.

Later that morning, after the worst of the spell had passed and her mother had slept with a shot of morphine, she took off her oxygen mask long enough to tell Jessica, "I can't talk, but I can listen to you talk."

Jessica sat beside her mother and tried to think of something to say, something that would be meaningful and would help ease her mother into death. But she ended up talking about nothing. Idle chat. A new welder she'd bought. A burn on her arm. Her department chair slamming the desk when she complained about her schedule. The new car she was thinking about buying. Caleb's work picking up and the house needing paint. That had seemed to satisfy her mother, even though it left Jessica disappointed. As her mother finally slipped into unconsciousness and died, Jessica realized that she and her mother had never talked about anything important.

As she thought back on her mother's death, Jessica felt the cold creeping over her, even though she had been perfectly warm before the phone rang. The lingering cold of the hospital room returned, the way it always did when she thought about her mother. She made sure the doors were locked and went upstairs to the bathroom, turned on the faucets on the tub, and watched the water steam. She never wanted to watch anything like her mother's death again as long as she lived.

That was part of the reason she was glad she left Caleb, although she knew that it would be impossible to explain. Caleb would be watching his father die soon, and even though she didn't particularly like the old man, she couldn't watch it. That part, at least, Caleb could understand, if she ever found a way to tell him.

Caleb didn't want to go through the pictures, but finally, he climbed the stairs and took the shoebox down from the closet shelf. The words "Family Pictures" were scrawled across the lid in fading magic marker, his mother's handwriting. The box felt too empty, even for his family. There had been some good times—maybe not Kodak moments, but enough to warrant more weight than he found in this little box.

Hubert had never cared for pictures, and after his wife died, there was hardly any family record.

The pictures were a mix of sharp old black and whites, grainy instamatic color shots, and faded Polaroids. Caleb scattered them across the bed and sorted through them. There were almost no pictures of his mother. They were mostly Hubert and Caleb dressed in their Sunday suits, standing in front of his parents' house, waiting for church. It was the only time Hubert would stand still long enough to have a picture snapped. He frowned in most of the pictures, or else looked distracted. Caleb just looked uncomfortable. All of those pictures he placed back in the box.

Near the bottom of the pile were a couple of pictures of his mother. One, taken when she was five or six years old, showed a skinny blonde girl smiling around missing front teeth. Her dress had ribbons at the shoulder and she was clutching a cloth doll with a porcelain face. The other picture showed her as a teenager perched on the fender of an old tractor that one of her brothers was driving across a field in Alabama.

She had been pretty, carefree. Caleb set those two aside, thinking that he ought to buy some nice frames and set them out in the living room. The only pictures displayed in the house were of Jessica's family.

He decided on one picture that had been taken on a fishing trip to the Tennessee River, up where it cut the northeast corner of the state. Caleb had been six or seven, but he remembered the trip because it was so unusual for the family to travel. It was a family reunion for Caleb's mother's family. For reasons that were still a mystery to Caleb, Hubert had refused to stay with any of his wife's people. So they'd camped at a state park on the river, where they fished all night and then went to see people during the day. Those people were all strangers to Caleb. He'd met most of his uncles, aunts, and cousins on that one trip. The other time he'd seen them was when they drove down for his mother's funeral.

The picture was a good one, though, and Caleb knew that it was the only one he would ever find that showed Hubert anything like happy. They had camped on a hill above the river, which Caleb remembered thinking was as big as the ocean. At that time he'd never been as far as Biloxi. Every night they would fish with jug lines—a hook and weight suspended from old Clorox bottles spray painted fluorescent orange— baiting them with minnows and setting them out in the river's current, where they would float all night. Hubert and Caleb would float along with the jugs, lighting them with the spotlight to see if a fish had struck. Once Hubert had pointed a spotlight at distant banks, dark lines of forest rising out of the water. "That's Mississippi," he said, then swung the light.

"That's Alabama. Tennessee is up that way a couple of miles."

Alabama and Tennessee sounded like exotic places to Caleb, places that he could name the capitols and university mascots, but they were just as distant as England or China. The nights were quiet and the sky was full. Floating around in that darkness, with only the glow of Hubert's cigarette and the occasional drone of barges being pushed along the river, Caleb had imagined that he might be lost on the ocean. He remembered being scared, and eventually he fell asleep on the life jackets in the bottom of the boat. In the morning they retrieved all the jugs, some of which they'd had to chase down as they were pulled along by catfish as long as Caleb's arm. As they pulled up to the bank and Caleb jumped out to tie off the boat, his mother had stepped from behind a tree, catching Hubert unaware. The picture showed him sitting in the back of the boat next to the motor, leaned forward over a box of orange jugs with a forearm on each knee, looking straight at the camera. The water behind him was smooth as glass and tinged red by the rising sun. Hubert almost looked happy, but he hadn't seen the camera until after the picture was taken. Caleb looked at the picture a long time before tucking it into his shirt pocket.

She stared at the panel, her sculpture, planted on the loading dock behind the fine arts building. What had once appeared to Jessica as a clear vision of the town lying under the hill where the Mississippi river cut a path between two states, now just seemed like amorphous layers of jagged metal tacked together with weak welds that wouldn't hold the seams of a ship together against the pressure exerted by a bathtub. In the loading bay beyond the dock, fraternity and sorority kids were building floats on flatbed trailers, getting an early start on new student orientation. They had erected two-by-four structures and molded shapes of people, buildings, and Greek letters out of chicken wire, which they would later papier-mache.

Boys walked past bored campus cops in a Jeep Cherokee to sip beers from the coolers in their car trunks. The girls smoked cigarettes in the shadows. A few of the frat boys wore baggy skateboard style shorts, but most of them just wore jeans and shirts with brand names splashed across the front. The girls wore short skirts, tanks, and cut-off jeans. The styles of the Seventies were back, for the girls at least. Jessica hoped nothing would ever bring back the big hair and preppie styles of the Eighties. She didn't recognize any of her students in the crowd, thank god. The art majors didn't tend to join fraternities, and those who did would think building floats an insult.

But it looked like the frat kids were having fun, at least, and Jessica wondered when was the last time she could say that for herself. She stared at her sculpture. It just stood there, pretentious and awkward. It might as well be chicken wire and papier-mache, so at least it would have some color and dimension to it. She picked up a short-handled three-pound sledgehammer. She closed her eyes and opened them, trying to see what she had once seen in the sculpture, but it wasn't there. She tried another angle, closing and opening her eyes again, and again it wasn't there. She wondered what she had been thinking all those months. She wished Caleb had told her it was shit.

It didn't matter. She took a swing at a panel of clouds above the town and felt the welds give a little. The loading bay reverberated with the sound and a few of the kids looked her way, but no one seemed to think anything was wrong. She struck the sculpture again, making the whole mass vibrate and wrinkle and give off a sharp ring like a steel drum. She hit it again and again.

No matter how hard she hit the sculpture it wouldn't break apart, and each swing pissed her off more. She remembered high school and playing with her father's arc welder, the other girls whispering about her dirty nails and burned arms. Her teachers wouldn't look at anything not sketched or painted or shaped out of clay. Her father would show off some of her smaller pieces at the shipyards, and his friends would shake their heads and critique her welds. Most of the students were watching her now and Jessica just kept hitting, becoming more and more absorbed in destroying the sculpture, more and more frustrated as she failed. It felt good to swing the hammer, though, and as she went after the sculpture, she thought about Caleb and Hubert and the assholes writing letters and killing coyotes and the people in her department and the paper company polluting the river and the pall of smoke that lingered in the woods from the clearcuts. It felt good.

She stopped, out of breath, her arm hanging at her side. The muscles in her right arm and shoulder burned, and she shifted the hammer to her left hand while she caught her breath. A big kid walked up onto the dock and picked up another hammer and tested the weight. He had on a pink knit shirt and wore his ball cap with the bill facing backwards.

"You need some help, Ma'am?" he asked. "It looks like fun." Jessica looked at him, confused. Her ears ringing.

The kid lifted his shoulders in a sort of question. He held the sledge like a baseball bat. He nodded at the sculpture again. "Mind if I have a go?"

Jessica registered what he was saying. She stepped between the kid and her sculpture. "I'm a professor, not a Ma'am."

He gave her a blank look, then flicked his eyes over the sculpture.

"Get off my dock," she said.

"What?"

Jessica took a step toward him, raising her hammer.

"I just thought you might need some help," he said. The kid backed away, his eyes wide. "It looked like fun."

"Get the fuck off my dock," she yelled. People stared at her, laughing and pointing. The kid left. The campus cops turned on their red and blue lights and painted the bay in flashing colors for a few seconds, but they seemed unsure of what had happened and turned the lights off without ever getting out of the car. The flashing lights seemed to calm the frat kids, and they turned back to their floats.

"I don't need any help," Jessica said. She looked at her sculpture. The welds were better than she had thought, and the hammering had added some texture. The slight waves and dents gave it a new depth. Jessica smiled at nothing in particular. She put her tools away in the toolbox and locked it, then walked toward her car.

It stormed all night, with heavy lightning and thunder giving way to a light drizzle. Caleb dreamed that he was back in his bedroom in his father's house. There were no locked doors in Hubert's house, and he woke Caleb by barging into his room just before daylight. The door opened with a noisy hardware ring that woke him instantly, and by the time Hubert said "get up" Caleb's feet were already on the floor and he was heading for the bathroom. In Caleb's dream the door kept opening and he would wake and stand, but his father was never there.

He had gotten up during the storm and stood on the porch, watching the lightning flashes illuminate sheets of horizontal rain, listening to water pour off the roof. He thought about God, and how he had once been convinced that God walked the earth during thunderstorms. God walking, shaking and lighting the earth with thunder and lightning. He thought about going to get the wolves and walking in the storm, but it was hard to move off the porch and the comfort of the cool damp breeze.

Just before dawn Caleb pulled on a clean pair of jeans and a flannel shirt. The storm had been driven ahead of a cold front. The rain had stopped except for the soft drip from trees, and the day would be clear and sunny, warm, with low humidity. He went to the kitchen and started coffee in graying light, then walked into the front room to find his boots. Hubert stood on the front porch, his back turned to the window. Caleb sat on the couch in the dark and watched Hubert while he tied his boots and waited for the coffee to finish. Hubert stood with both hands in his pockets and shoulders hunched. His head tucked into his shoulders like a dove trying to roost. He looked fragile, and Caleb wondered if the cancer was already working on his body, or if knowing about the cancer made him see his father differently. He thought that maybe that was the way cancer worked, not so much physical as mental. Just the word inspired fear.

Caleb knew his father had been up for hours, straightening out any possible disorder that might have occurred at his house overnight. He would have already seen to his cattle and his catfish ponds. He had probably already driven his garbage to the dump and made a couple more changes to his will.

He had called Caleb's house to ask for a ride to chemotherapy. That must have taken a bite out of his pride. It bothered Caleb in ways that made him feel guilty, but it had taken him years to get out from under his father's weight, and he was afraid of slipping back into the little boy who tried so hard to please his father, but never seemed quite able.

Hubert turned a little. His lips moving, probably wondering aloud how a grown man could still be asleep and it almost daylight. Caleb crept closer to the open window, keeping in the shadows.

"Lord, you know I don't feel Your presence in that place like I do out here. I can't find You there. All those chemicals. I don't blame You for forsaking that place. I want to die in the world you made. I'm only doing it for my son, and I want You to make him start thinking about how he's lived his life. Promise me You don't let me die in that place. Let me die at home, on my own land. Let me die with a little dignity.

Hubert turned and looked in the window. "Good god boy. You'd sleep half the day if someone didn't watch out for you."

He walked back to his pickup and opened the door and pressed the horn.

Caleb walked back to the kitchen and poured a cup of coffee and leaned against the sink. Hubert had never been afraid of anything in his life, but it made sense to be afraid of dying in a hospital. Caleb hadn't been to church in years, but he liked the idea of an all-powerful, omnipotent God who was driven out of the hospitals by Pine-sol, a god who chose to live in the woods and fields.

The horn started Max and Lulu howling from the pen. The sound angered Hubert, and he leaned on the horn, trying to drown the wolves out. Finally he gave up and stomped to the door and banged. He had always been good in the mornings, eager and full of energy, ready to set the world back on its foundation. As a child, Caleb dreaded the mornings because his father set such a pace. But as Hubert aged he flagged in the afternoons, his aches and age catching up to him, and he would work out his pain on whoever happened to be handy. But in the mornings he was a wonder to watch, a man to watch out for.

Caleb filled his thermos with coffee and turned off the machine, then slipped out the back door. He walked into the woods and circled around to the wolf pen trail, then started back to the house.

"What the hell are you doing?"

Hubert jumped, then recovered. "Can't you give a man a whoop once in a while, let him know you're in the woods?"

"You were making too much noise to hear it," Caleb said. "Come in and sit down for a while. You've got a long day ahead of you."

Hubert had looked okay after his first chemo treatment, but Caleb wondered when the change would come. How long would he keep his weight and hair? Already, he thought that Hubert's skin seemed tighter in his face, and his color had gone almost yellow.

"No," he said. "I'm going to run over to the church and make sure the bathrooms are clean. I probably won't feel much like it afterwards."

Caleb poured coffee into his thermos cup and blew on it to cool. He shook his head. "You really need to be doing that today?"

"We're supposed to be there by nine," Hubert said.

"I can clean the toilets for you."

Hubert gave him a long look. "I don't reckon they want the church to burn down when lightning strikes it."

Caleb turned the thermos upside down to check the mouth for leaks. "You know, it wouldn't hurt you to be more appreciative. Neither one of us has a lot going for us, and you're worse off than me.

Hubert turned and headed for his truck, then stopped. "Well," he said. He stared into the woods growing a soft gray with the coming morning, then dropped his head and sorted through his keyring. "I might hold you to it in a few weeks. But I'm not that sick yet." He started back toward his pickup. "Come by the church and drive me to town."

Caleb watched him drive away, then headed down the path toward the wolf pen.

Max and Lulu were edgy, spooked by the horn, and no amount of coaxing could ease them. Lulu crouched in a submissive posture, tail tucked and belly to the ground as she stared at a spot in the woods outside the pen. When Caleb knelt to soothe her, she let out a low growl and flashed her canines. Max cast a look at the same area that was bothering Lulu and cut out for deep cover.

Caleb pulled his pistol and walked towards the spot the wolves had pointed, a slight rise topped by a thicket of holly and saw briars. There he found some matted grass where something or someone had bedded down for a while and a few marks that could have been boots, but he wasn't enough of a tracker to say yes or no. Whatever it was had gone, although probably not for long. He walked a grid pattern around the spot, finding nothing, until it was time to leave to meet his father.

Max and Lulu spooked when the horn blew at the house. Jessica wondered what was happening, but she was also glad because it meant she wouldn't have to see Caleb. The wolves stood by the gate and watched her approach. Their ears stood straight and their tails switched slightly, but they bolted as she reached for the latch. The move both surprised and hurt her. She had imagined a joyful reunion. At first she hoped it was only the storm that passed through, spooking them, but then she admitted that it was her that had them out of sorts. She'd been gone too long for them to act as if nothing had happened.

Leaving Max and Lulu had been the hardest part of leaving Caleb. She crouched by the gate and waited, watching for Lulu's ears or tail or a flash of color to appear through the brush. After several minutes the quiet of her disturbance passed and birds began to chirp and squirrels rattled the branches of the longleaf pines again. A flick of movement deep in the pen turned Jessica's head and she caught a glimpse of Lulu slinking behind a patch of big-leaf magnolia. Knowing that Max used Lulu as a diversion, Jessica whirled and saw him vanish into a stand of saw briars and cane thirty yards away.

Fifteen minutes later the wolves had worked no closer to her. Disappointed, Jessica leaned against the fence and closed her eyes. She had worried that leaving the wolves for so long might damage their trust, but she still wasn't prepared to see it in action. Not for the first time, she wondered if leaving the wolves had been another in a long line of mistakes she'd made with Caleb.

She wasn't sure what to do, but then she heard someone coming down the trail to the pen. She slipped out the gate and into the woods. At the top of the hill she crouched behind cover and watched him approach the pen. He seemed distracted, and a little beaten down, and she remembered that he was going to be with his father for the chemo treatments. It took a few moments before he appeared to notice the odd behavior of the wolves, but when he did she backed into the woods and headed for home.

Hubert crawled onto the church pew from his hands and knees and sat. The seat was littered with gum wrappers and church attendance cards covered with scribbling. He had been trying to vacuum, but the machine didn't have enough power to pick up the mess left behind by the high school kids who sat in a pew in the front, where their parents could watch them during the service and keep them out of trouble.

There were enough attendance cards to supply the church for a month, wasted, whining about boredom and how long the sermon was going to last, wondering "what would Jesus do if he had to listen to this shit much longer," mixed in with the occasional book chapter and verse from the sermon. There were scrawled initials, words that Hubert couldn't make sense of, and drawings of cars and trees and faces. Hubert shook his head at one drawing of a naked woman, her breasts the size of watermelons, before dropping it in the trash can.

Caleb acted the same way when he was a boy. During services Hubert stood in the back of the auditorium next to the double doors, his hands folded before him, his eyes watching the young people who always sat in the front left pews. There always seemed to be seven or eight kids whose parents allowed them enough freedom to sit as a group during Sunday preaching, and for the most part they were well behaved. But sooner or later Hubert would see one boy's elbow go into the ribs of the boy beside him, then it would spread down

the pew like a stack of falling dominoes before working back to the boy who had started it. Hubert would
make his way to the front of the building and quietly
take a seat behind the boys. Immediately, the foolish-
ness would stop, but as soon as the invitation song
was sung and the last prayer uttered, Hubert would
squeeze Caleb's arm and tell him to go wait outside in
the pickup.

Kids needed to be shown how they should act, and
he had never backed down from settling Caleb on the
straight and narrow. Parents that didn't care enough
about their kids to give them a slap on the cheek or a
switch across the legs, needed a whipping themselves.
Letting these hellions disrespect the house of God by
scattering cookie crumbs and wrappers and sticking
their gum under the pew to dry, and all the time the
parents moaning about the schools not doing their
jobs anymore and their kids didn't have any principles
or morals and were so concerned about texting and
tweeting and God knows what else on phones that
cost a thousand dollars.

Hubert remembered going to church before there
was a building, his mother waking him, washing him
and threatening to beat him if he got his clothes dirty,
and then walking to Uncle Henry's house, where Old
man Stevenson would preach, sometimes for three
hours before his voice gave out on him. The women
made a pot of stew and cornbread, or fried three or
four chickens if it was a special occasion, and after all
the men had filled their plates, and the women theirs,
the kids got to eat. They met in one house or another
for what seemed like forever, until the congregation
put together a little money and bought an acre in thick
woods that they cleared out and made into a church.

They called it the Brush Arbor. There wasn't a building for the longest time. On Saturdays the men would go down to the arbor and cut trees, leaving the stumps knee high. They ripped planks out of the logs with handsaws and nailed the planks across the stumps to make pews. To cover the pews they erected posts and strung ropes and wire and wove the leaf and needle covered branches through the ropes to make an arbor.

Because of the weather, they couldn't meet every Sunday, especially during winter. But when they did meet it would go on all day, and when the work season allowed, they'd meet every day for a week or two. Preaching would start in the morning and go until lunch, when they'd spread blankets on the ground and eat a picnic. Then preaching would start back up and go on until everyone was hungry again, or dark coming on.

He still dreamed about those Sundays. The smell of fresh cut pine planks sharp and resinous sometimes woke him at night. His mother spread burlap bags so the pitch wouldn't stick to their clothes. The sound of flies buzzing the food packed away in baskets and covered by towels. The rolling voices of the preachers with the big bellies and long beards who stood on the stump platform at the head of the arbor and condemned and shouted and prayed and sweated until their clothes were so soaked it didn't matter when they waded into the creek to baptize. The smell of the dark water when he was himself baptized and raised back into the air of the world, redeemed, the current flowing toward the Gulf of Mexico, diluting his sins until they were harmless, filtering them through gravel and sand shoals. The sound of a light breeze sifting through the arbor, whispering through the leaves like

the angels ministering to Jesus after forty days of fast-
ing and praying and resisting the devil's temptations
in the desert.

Sometimes Hubert wondered what it would have
been like if his father had lived long enough to know
him. His mother always said his father was a good
man, a good Christian, even though he refused to miss
a day logging to go to preaching. His father could work
a team of horses. With just two small draft horses,
his father could skid logs out of the woods almost as
quick as any diesel skidder Caterpillar ever rolled out
of Peoria, and without tearing up the woods nearly
as bad.

But a tree that fell the wrong way ended that, and
Hubert's mother never had any luck with men after
her first husband died. Hubert's stepfather did little
more than drink and beat up his mother. He didn't
start out so bad, but it got worse as Hubert got older.

It wasn't every night. Sometimes he and his mother
and Victor lived a normal life for weeks at a time. But
eventually Victor would start to drink. Hubert woke
to screaming and slurred curses, the wicked sound of
hand meeting flesh and his mother falling. Sometimes
Hubert would run in to try and help his mother, only
for Victor to start on him. Other nights, his mother
would wake just in time to wrap a blanket around him
and run out the door to hide. Lying in the weeds of
the ditch, the sounds of the horse team—his father's
horses, their traces jingling and the creak of the leather
harnesses and the groan of the flat-bed wagon bear-
ing the drunken sot home to take out his frustrations
on his wife and adopted child. They would lie there,
mother and child, in the mud and ditch water, until
the man finished searching the house and started back

along the road looking for them. That was another part of his dreams that woke him still, the smell of ditch water. Then they would fade back into the trees, into the blackness of the shadows, waiting until Victor stumbled on past them. Hubert still, after fifty years, favored moonless nights because it reminded him of the times when the light made it difficult to hide.

The hospital had grown since Caleb was a child. Each addition featured a new design, so the mix of red brick and steel and glass made it difficult to guess the age of the building. Caleb dropped off Hubert and looked for a parking spot. Visitors looking lost and distressed, and staff dressed in green, purple, and pink scrubs and white lab coats, walked in and out of the entrance. None of the faces he knew, which struck him as strange since he'd grown up near town, had gone to high school and college there, and had covered stories during the health care debates.

Outside the entrance a man in a hospital gown sat in a wheelchair and smoked a cigarette. His wife sat on the curb beside him with her hands draped over her knees. Caleb nodded and walked on through, but neither looked at him. The inside of the hospital had also changed over the years. Originally a rectangular building with a central hall, now the polished steel and glass entrance led into an older section built in the 1940s that used radiated heat. Another turn might lead to a section built somewhere in between and starting to show wear. It took him a series of turns to find where they had tacked on the oncology unit.

Hubert leaned against the counter in the waiting room, talking to the receptionist through the sliding glass window. He looked up at Caleb.

"We been waiting."

Caleb looked at his watch. "It's straight up nine."

"Well," Hubert said. Then he turned to the woman. "This is my boy, such as he is. I'm ready when you are."

The receptionist looked at Caleb. "Would you like to go in with your father while he has his treatment?"

"He'll wait out here," Hubert said.

"You can both have a seat," she said. Then to Caleb, she said "It'll be a couple of hours. We have a cafeteria if you want to go get breakfast."

"That's fine," Caleb said. "I'll just wait here."

They sat in the waiting area and Hubert just glared at him, so Caleb picked up a magazine. After a few minutes a nurse led Hubert back through the doors.

Caleb put the magazine down and slumped in his chair. The furniture was nicely upholstered—it hadn't had time to draw coffee stains or to wear. The television was tuned to the *Today Show.* Waiting in the room, there were a couple of old women dressed nice enough for church, and an old man in overalls. Caleb's clothes smelled of diesel and wolf.

The receptionist came over to Caleb and handed him a cup of coffee in a tiny styrofoam cup. She was middle-aged with heavy makeup. He took the cup and thanked her.

"You didn't come in with your father before," she said, sitting down.

"No. He wouldn't have it before now."

"He's going to need a lot of support. I brought you some literature for you to read." She handed Caleb a stack of pamphlets.

"Thank you. I'll get started on these right away."

"He really needs you," the woman reminded him. "He might not say it, but he does." She went back to her desk and looked at her computer.

Caleb sorted through the pamphlets: "A Guide to Chemotherapy," "For Families of Cancer Patients," "When Cancer Strikes Your Family." There were more. Caleb stuck the pamphlets in his shirt pocket and stared back at the television, but the volume was too low to hear what the announcers were saying. He looked back at the woman behind the glass.

Caleb didn't remember anything like this when his mother was dying in the hospital. There weren't any pamphlets saying what was happening or how to help. Just Bible tracts handed out by the preacher. Some women from church. His mother lived in the Intensive Care Unit, and Caleb stayed in the waiting room whenever his father was allowed to go back and see her. Whenever his father left, the preacher or one of the other men from the church had always seemed uncomfortable to be left alone with Caleb. They ignored him when his father was there, but as soon as Hubert left the room the old preacher would suddenly feel the need to pray, and he would make Caleb kneel in a tight circle with whoever else was waiting.

Caleb wasn't ready for the hospital. He got up and took a chair in the corner, as far away from the other people as he could get, and watched the *Today Show* end. What came on next was a program with a man and woman drinking coffee from soup-bowl mugs. The waiting room was starting to fill up. He wasn't ready for his father's sickness, he didn't want to talk about God, he didn't want to think about his mother, and he didn't want to think about Jessica. A look at his watch showed a long time yet to wait, so he got up and walked out of the waiting room. The receptionist gave him a look as he walked toward the door. He patted the pamphlets in his shirt pocket.

NATCHEZ AT SUNSET ~ 97

The strip mall had been new in the 1970s; in-between the malls lay mom and pop used car lots and old houses that had been turned into pawn shops and vacuum and cell phone repair businesses. A Mexican grocery had gone out of business, and the half dozen Mexican restaurants had gone out too following the crack-down on illegal immigrants. Same for the Chinese buffets. The Indian run motels were still doing well, the sidewalks outside the rooms decorated with children's toys, charcoal grills, and the parking lots holding two or three cars on blocks. Caleb drove into the country through pine forests that formed a roof over the two-lane going to cut over timber and clear cuts, aluminum trailers, fields of soybeans and corn, fields where the fruit that needed to be hand-picked rotted on the vine, and fields that hadn't been planted in the first place. He didn't think about where he was going. He took turns randomly as they came. He wondered what Jessica was doing. He thought about driving past her house, but didn't for fear of crowding her too much. He was worried about seeing her, or not seeing her, or what he would do if a strange car was parked out front.

After a while he wound up back in town, though he wasn't sure how he had gotten back. There were so many new roads that hadn't been there when he was a teenager and had spent every minute he could away from his father, mostly driving. Even on Friday and Saturday nights, when other kids his age went to movies and on dates and hung out at the city park, he'd driven alone, drinking beer he'd bought with a fake I.D. New subdivisions were going up and what had been country a few years ago was lined with convenience stores, small churches, and the occasional hair dresser working out of her garage. Caleb still had too much time before his father would be done. On a whim he pulled into a convenience store and bought a six pack and turned onto a road that he remembered should loop around to the north end of town. He opened a beer and sipped.

The day had warmed, and Caleb rolled the window down and hung his arm out. The air smelled like rotting leaves and earth. He turned into a old neighborhood where the houses were run down and weeds grew around cars parked in the yards. The houses were built on brick piling, and the streets made sharp turns to avoid a large creek that wound through the back yards. Caleb parked in front of a littered vacant lot with a free-standing chimney and got out to look at the creek.

The channel was thirty feet wide and ten deep, and it looked like people had been dumping there for years. There were concrete blocks, chunks of pavement, re-bar, shingles, rusted steel drums, car and truck tires, scraps of lumber and plywood sticking out at odd angles, and one old street sign that read SLOW CHURCH ZONE wedged into the debris.

A rusty brown current flowed around the junk, kicking up standing waves and small waterfalls. Caleb sat on the bank and watched some boys float aluminum cans in the shallows. He couldn't remember the last time that anything had seemed that simple.

Mr. Vogel had a rough treatment," the nurse said to Caleb. "He ought to stay here and rest a little longer. Maybe you could talk to him."

"Take me home," Hubert whispered. He sat in a wheelchair holding his stomach with both hands.

"It doesn't sound like a good idea."

"You can do it or I'll walk."

Caleb looked to the nurse for help. "Sometimes you have to become the parent."

Hubert muttered something and tried to stand up. Caleb grabbed his arm and eased him down.

"I'll take you home, then."

The nurse followed Caleb toward the door. "Are you an only child, Mr. Vogel?"

"Yes." She had a kind face.

"Do you have anyone you can talk to about your father? A pastor?"

"I've been through it before. My mother."

She smiled and nodded. "I see this a lot. Parents and children who don't understand that their roles have changed. You've got to make him understand that he's sick and that he's got to mind."

"You've seen my father."

She went back to Hubert and Caleb paused in the hallway, torn between telling the woman to mind her own business and sitting down with her for coffee so he could tell her the whole story.

After he pulled the truck around, the nurse helped Hubert into the cab, giving Caleb a sympathetic smile. Caleb started for the driver's side.

"Thanks," he said. He drove toward the highway.

Hubert sat up straight in the pickup and stared out the window, holding his stomach with both hands.

"What did the doctors tell you today?"

"Said I've got cancer."

"What else?"

"Said I'm going to die."

Caleb let off the gas and looked at him. "They said that?" "Not in so many words, but that's what it means when they stop talking to the sick person and start talking to the family. I know that from your mother."

He didn't say anything else, and when they got to his house, Caleb helped him into his chair.

"What do you need?" Caleb asked. "Nothing."

"You sure?"

"The cancer's in my lungs, not my brain." Caleb nodded and turned to leave.

"Hey," Hubert said. His face was pale. He grimaced. "Get me some water. And some toilet paper."

Caleb walked into the kitchen and filled a glass. In the bathroom he looked up and caught his reflection in the mirror above the sink. His face always surprised him. He pictured his hair fuller and his face thinner, no trace of gray in his beard, and his belly tight. He wondered what Jessica had thought as she watched him change. She had changed too, grown softer and grayer, and she had changed the way she thought about things. It was inevitable, but the hard part was there was no guarantee you liked the way the other person changed.

Caleb drove home, not wanting to be there. It seemed like such a long time since Jessica left, even though it had only been a couple of weeks. He missed the end of the day, the afternoons winding up in the shop, walking together to see the wolves, walking down to the river. He thought about how they really hadn't talked in a long time. Or had they ever talked? At home, Jessica never talked about school, her mother, or even her art. Caleb didn't talk about the newspaper, his father, politics. They both made a point of not talking about children.

When he pulled up to the house, Lulu began to bark. He listened to her, but after a while he decided this bark didn't mean anything, at least nothing that required action. But then he felt a pang of guilt. A wolf's bark always meant something. Fear, sometimes, and sometimes it meant happy, or lonely, or bored. Caleb hadn't spent much time with the wolves since Jessica had left, other than feeding them every day. There had been few walks, no rough-housing. It was more than just Jessica being gone; it was the way she had taken away the wolves when she had left.

People, including his father, had asked Caleb since the beginning what in the hell he thought he was doing trying to raise wolves in Mississippi. He talked about connecting to nature, preserving the land, vague ideas like that. There was some truth in it. There was something spiritual about the wolves too. He could see why the Indians and Eskimos held them in such awe, but deep down he knew that he wasn't that spiritual a person. He suspected that there were a lot of reasons to explain Max and Lulu, all of them a part of the whole. But all he really knew was that at some point he had begun to lose Jessica, and the wolves had kept her with him, at least for a couple of years. With the wolves, there was a better chance that Jessica would come home. That's all that mattered.

Stella's Coffee House wasn't crowded yet, except for a couple of kids slouching at a table and pecking away at laptops. Acoustic rock wafted above the noise of dishes in the kitchen and the barista steaming milk. Jessica ordered a latte and a chicken salad sandwich from the waitress, a girl who looked familiar. Jessica tried to remember if she'd ever had a class with the girl. She wasn't an art major, but she had the look of carefully put-together carelessness—the top and skirt that didn't quite go together but did, the headband holding her hair back in a tousled mess that must have taken some time to arrange. Perhaps the girl had taken one of the entry-level courses and changed majors after she found out she didn't like criticism or didn't want to put in the time. When the girl brought the sandwich she acted like she might start a conversation, but Jessica smiled and thanked her and retreated into a back room before she had a chance.

She chose a small room, probably one of the original bedrooms of the house, with a worn chair angled along a set of French doors and a small table with two empty chairs on the inside wall. The books on the shelves didn't appeal to her. She just wanted to sit and not think, not talk, just be. She selected a book at random and settled into the chair. She opened it on her lap to ward off conversation and stared out the window. The oaks ringing the patio cast a deep summer shade. The music was catchy enough to make Jessica think she could listen to this band, but like the waitress, it was too self-consciously hip to bother getting to know. She leaned over and opened her purse—a canvas shoulder bag she'd gotten at a military surplus in Montana—and took out a pen and a memo pad. She made a few notes about the opening for her exhibit: a list of small pieces to be included, a diagram of the arrangement of the pieces that would lead the viewers through all the works and build to the centerpiece, a guest list. There wasn't much work to the guest list, since all the art faculty openings were open to the public. However, the department would send out invitations to the college deans, the president and chancellor and other university officials, and to a few alumni, big donors who supported the arts. She was supposed to add names to the list. Family. Friends. Caleb.

She wrote out his name and address. It looked strange—her address and his name. She'd never addressed anything to him. She'd never even written his name on the return address of an envelope. She drew some geometric shapes around his name and address and colored them in with her pen. The last exhibit Caleb had attended was a visiting printmaker from Arkansas. Caleb struggled. He could interview anybody, but without focusing questions, he had no more patience for small talk than did Hubert. It wasn't just a matter of filling in the gaps with idle conversation. He wore the scent of the wolves on his body—a musky worn-in smell that didn't wash off and even diesel and oil exhaust couldn't mask. Jessica knew she had it too —the faint trace of burnt metal breathed in and exiting through her pores. She never noticed it or thought about it unless she was staying in town for a few days, or not working. She wondered if anyone ever wanted to mention it to her but was too polite. Caleb ended up standing near the food line or beside the bar, sipping a beer and nodding at anyone he made eye contact with.

She didn't know if he would even come, and she wasn't ready to talk about their situation. How would he interpret an invitation? How would he feel about not being invited at all? She still didn't know what she wanted to happen. She wrote a question mark beside his name, then tore the page out of her notebook and dropped it inside her bag.

The Natchez piece was almost finished. There were a few more touches to be made. She wasn't sure how to present it, but she was thinking a simple black fabric backdrop. She would experiment. It hadn't turned out the way she had envisioned it, but then none of her pieces ever did. It was dark, darker that she had planned. The clouded sky above the bluff, layered copper sheets, had absorbed a lot of her sadness over the last few months. The little town nestled under the Mississippi River bluffs was cut off from the rest of the world, bounded by sedimentary rock on one side and a rushing, swirling river on the other.

The Louisiana bank across the river from Natchez was where she had found herself one evening after a long day of following two-lane highways and county roads in an easterly direction. She'd drive until forced to turn or backtrack, and at intersections she made choices on a whim. She'd begun that day, two years ago, in New Orleans, standing beside the bed of a teenage girl—Lacey—who had delivered a baby girl during the night. Lacey had dropped out of St. Luke's High school in Algiers. She wanted her baby to go to a "good Christian couple." Jessica and Caleb were contacted by the adoption agency, for some reason, even though Jessica hadn't seen the inside of a church since her mother died—at least four years—and Caleb longer than that. But they could still talk church, and they'd lied about their faith when they met Lacey in her parent's living room for the initial interview and had passed inspection. Lacey's mother told Jessica over and over how good a mother Jessica would make now that God had given her a child. She'd told Jessica that Sarah in the Old Testament was a wonderful mother, despite the barren womb that God eventually cured. Adoption was just the way God chose to work in Jessica's case, the woman told her.

Jessica hadn't felt bad about lying to Lacey. For years she sat in church and listened to others talk about how God had blessed them. New jobs were answered prayers. Illnesses healed and pregnancies achieved; safe trips, promotions, and the booming economy; the election of Republican presidents; and even the winner of the Ole Miss – State game: all were interpreted as the direct hand of God intervening in the lives of faithful Christians. Jessica had dropped off Facebook, unable to read another post that ended with #blessed, and she glared helplessly at cashiers and bank tellers who ended every transaction with "have a blessed day."

She had gone to services, prayed, and most of the time tried to be a good person, and still she sat beside a hospital bed and watched her mother die, ruined her credit running to Jackson and spreading her legs for the infertility clinic, and drained her marriage of intimacy. Where was God then? She had quit praying, quit believing, quit trying to convince God how badly she needed this child.

She knew Caleb wasn't thrilled about adoption. She knew her unhappiness had forced this on him.

Proof of his love. She didn't know what it was about men, the need to know their children were their own before they could care. How badly had his infertility wrecked his self-confidence? Enough to make him go through so many cycles of in vitro. Unwilling to give up. Once the doctors refused another cycle, though, he bucked up. He kept coming up with the money for an adoption. Writing article after article; picking up free-lance pieces; moving earth on the side, late at night, working under floodlights. He took a liking to Lacey, joking with her about not being able to understand her thick accent, buying her things to help her through the pregnancy. A used iPhone so she could post selfies of her expanding belly. DVDs and new clothes. A laptop for when she got ready to go back to school. He even got on Facebook for a while. On one trip back from New Orleans to check on Lacey, Caleb pulled off at a shopping center and they went in to look for a crib and nursery furniture. The concept of a baby grew from an abstraction to something real, each time Lacey shared an ultrasound image or recorded the baby's heartbeat on her phone, but Jessica wondered if Caleb knew how much his life was going to change, or how he would feel once it really did change.

Lacey's mother called late one afternoon and told Jessica that Lacey had gone into premature labor. Jessica hadn't waited for Caleb to come home from work. She tried to call but service was spotty, so she scrawled a note and left it on the kitchen table and sped to New Orleans, calling and leaving messages for Caleb, praying hard all the way for Lacey and the little girl. Christy, she'd already decided to name her.

A labor and delivery nurse led her to Lacey's room. As she walked along the white corridors, Jessica remembered her mother, another hospital. Lacey—seven and a half months. Not long enough. It couldn't be accurate. The OB had made a mistake dating the conception. Caleb's fucking phone—a new phone for Lacey and half the time his piece of shit didn't get service. She'd left the paperwork on her dresser, too rushed to think about the signatures she needed from Lacey's parents. Seven and a half months. That couldn't be right. Too early.

Lacey's mother and grandmother sat on either side of Lacey's bed. Each nodded to Jessica but neither made room for her. The mother's lips were set in a thin line, the grandmother looked ready to chew up an intern or a nurse, or anybody handy. The girl looked more scared than in pain. Her hair was sweat-damp and wild, her face pale and desperate, eyes of a little girl facing grown-up pain. She looked so young. Jessica stood at the foot of the bed. She wanted to reach out and pat Lacey's leg. Somebody ought to touch her, hold her, so she wasn't going through this alone. Why hadn't she picked up flowers, at least, so she'd have something to do with her hands?

"How are you?" Jessica asked, but Lacey looked toward the window and grimaced through a contraction. "How is she?" Jessica directed the question toward Lacey's mother.

The mother shrugged, not looking at Jessica, and finally caressed her daughter's head, an afterthought. "It's only going to get worse from here on out, Baby."

Lacey arched in the bed, her feet rattling the stirrups. "My cooter," she said. "It hurts, Mama!"

The grandmother looked at Jessica. "I taught her to call it her cooter."

Jessica smiled and nodded. She wished she'd called the lawyer before she left home.

The labor went on for the rest of the afternoon and late into the evening. Nurses, technicians, and doctors trooped in and out of the room, scanning charts and the readouts on the monitors. Someone brought in a Styrofoam cup with ice chips and placed it on the bedside table. A nurse checked the fetal heart rate monitor strapped to Lacey's abdomen, put on a pair of surgical gloves and measured how far she was dilated. She patted Lacey's leg. "Y'ain't ready yet, Honey. Just got to hang in there a little longer."

Jessica excused herself and followed the nurse out the door. "Is the baby okay?" she asked.

"Who're you?" She was a wiry red head with a smoker's cough. Her name tag read "Shiree."

"I'm adopting the baby."

"Hmmm. Well. It ain't none of my business, but you don't need to be in there."

Jessica stepped back. "Why shouldn't I be here?"

Shiree set her hands on her hips and squared off on Jessica. "Two things: That little baby in there is hurting and scared and you ain't her Mama. She looks up and sees you standing at the foot of her bed looking like a hungry bird ready to pick up the child she's been carrying and crying and hurting over for so long. Make her liable to change her mind. You get on out to the waiting room and leave that girl alone. Let her Mama take care of her."

"We've got all the papers drawn up and ready to be signed. We're paying all her bills."

"I've seen it happen," Shiree said. "Woman gets mighty protective about her baby once she sees it and holds it, hears it scream and cry and latch on."

Jessica folded her arms. "You said two things."

Shiree sighed. She looked up and down the hall-way, then whispered. "That baby's in trouble. Heart rate decelerating. Underweight and premature. That girl's not going to deliver vaginally. They getting an emergency C-section ready." She touched Jessica's arm. "We been trying to get an ambulance or a heli-copter to take her to the NICU at St. Josephs. A real NICU, but that girl don't got insurance and so this is where you go when you don't got insurance."

Jessica felt like she was having to translate from another language. "We're paying her bills. We've got it all figured out on a time plan."

Shiree shook her head and said, "St. Jo don't know about no time plan." She walked off and, passing an-other nurse, said loudly, "I didn't say nothing."

Jessica stood in the hallway for a few minutes, then stepped back into the room. She ran her hand tenderly along Lacey's ankle. "I'm sorry if I'm in the way. I'll be out in the waiting area if you need me for anything."

Lacey gave Jessica a vacant stare and Lacey's mother smiled graciously and told her thank you. She promised to call Jessica when the time was closer.

No one would talk to her about Lacey at the nurse's station. "If you ain't family, we can't say noth-ing about her finances, about her baby, about noth-ing." Jessica walked toward the administrative offices, but couldn't find anyone to talk to her. She picked up a cup of coffee at the cafeteria, then returned to the waiting area. A Hispanic man and three children waited in one corner. The children played quietly on the floor and the man kept his eyes glued to a Spanish language station on the television above the wall. The waiting room was cramped and the magazines were out of date. Jessica couldn't get comfortable. The room felt dirty. She imagined germs and viruses and molecules of disease wafting through the ventilation system, settling on the furniture and walls and floors, seeping into her skin.

She had been so cold the night before her mother died.

She'd wrapped herself in a coarse hospital blanket, the room lit by monitors and a flickering and buzzing fluorescent light from the crack beneath the bathroom door. Her mother in and out of consciousness. In her lucid moments, she complained she was burning up. The nurse told Jessica it was because her mother was working so hard to breathe. Around two a.m. she took off her oxygen mask and told Jessica, "I've got to make it to morning." Her face, wasted by the cancer, was contorted from the pain and the demons from her hallucinations. Her veins had deteriorated so she couldn't keep an IV open, and she was scheduled for a procedure to put in a permanent IV. She didn't want pain medicine anyway.

Jessica sat on a cot beside the bed, dozing and starting. Around four her mother dropped off to sleep, but ten minutes later a nurse's aid came in to weigh her. She was so short she could barely see above the bed and talked like she had gravel in her mouth. She moved the bed up and down, jerking Jessica's mother back into consciousness, and then left. A few minutes later another nurse came in to take blood. She worked both arms and both hands, tapping for a vein, poking her over and over with needles but never hitting anything. Jessica sat on the cot and watched. The nurse ignored her; she seemed as caught up in her work as any artist over a canvas. Jessica's mother stared at the nurse over her oxygen mask, wild-bird eyed, until finally the nurse left having accomplished nothing.

Jessica shook off the memory of her mother and wondered what was happening with Lacey as she wandered past patient rooms catching snatches of TV and wondering why none of the other visitors she saw in the hallways looked as lost as she felt. She wondered where Caleb was as she made a fourth round past the nurse's station and looked for Lacey's nurse, but the nurse wasn't there and no one else offered help her. In the lobby she stopped by a bank of pay telephones and tried to remember when she had last used one. She walked outside into the sunlight and called Caleb. No answer. She called Hubert and he dismissed her, saying he hadn't seen his son and no, he was too busy to go looking for him. She ended with a call to the lawyer, Jim, but it was after five and all she could do was leave a message.

Jessica wondered who she could call next. There was no one she needed to call, but working the phone felt positive. It was what people did, waiting at the hospital. But now, she thought about how she had no one else to call—no minister, no girlfriends, no mother or father, not even anyone from her department she felt close enough to share this moment in her life. Back inside, she stared at the bank of phones and wondered how she had ever managed to make herself so completely alone in the world.

It wasn't long after that a flurry of activity erupted around Lacey's room. Several of the hospital staff pushed in a gurney, gowned for the operation. A few minutes later they wheeled Lacey out. She was crying, her face broken. The mother and grandmother shuffled out behind her, both crying, and neither bothering to speak to Lacey. The grandmother railed on the nearest staff, a tiny black woman who looked ready to claw the old woman's eyes out. The whole bunch disappeared through a set of automatic doors under a sign that kept out visitors. Jessica went back to the waiting area and stared at her phone.

Caleb got to the hospital around eleven that evening, having worked until dark. He said he'd only found her note as he ate a ham sandwich over the sink, staring out the window and wondering where she was out to so late. He'd tried to call but the call kept dropping. He had more questions than Jessica could answer. She told him about what the nurse had said to her earlier in the afternoon, checking off the details in short sentences.

"Let me call Jim," Caleb said, standing. He sounded tired. Jessica watched him go. Too little, too late, Jessica thought. He came back a few minutes later and shook his head and sat down beside Jessica with his elbows on his knees and his chin in his hands, his classic waiting pose—something he didn't do well. Jessica didn't want to be near him. She walked back and forth in front of the nurse's station, but the staff continued to ignore her. At seven in the morning, Lacey's mother walked into the waiting room. Jessica stirred from a light sleep and watched her approach. Her body didn't respond immediately, even though Jessica wanted to jump to her feet and grab the woman by the shoulders and shake her for news, shake her for leaving her to wonder all night. Jessica felt both heavy and weightless at the same time, as if it wasn't really her body that she inhabited. She eased out of the chair and waited, trying to gauge the impassive expression on the mother's face.

Lacey's mother looked worn. She stared at Jessica for a long time, as if placing blame and weighing her words. Jessica knew that she was about to be told that Lacey had decided to keep the baby, and her mother didn't know how to break the news. Her mind raced through her options. She wanted to hurt something, someone.

"It was a little girl," Lacey's mother started, "three pounds and six ounces."

"What?"

"It was too early. Her lungs, they didn't work right. Her lungs." She shifted a cloth shopping bag from one shoulder to the other. "They took the baby, but it was too late. Or too early."

Jessica dropped to her knees. She felt Caleb's arms on her shaking shoulders. She felt Lacey's mother's stare.

"They moving Lacey to the third floor," the mother said, eyeing Caleb. "She might be here a day or two."

Caleb nodded. The air rushed out of Jessica's lungs. She sank into a tunnel, and everything went dark.

She listened to Caleb talk in a low voice to Lacey's mother. "We want you to tell Lacey that we're very sorry," she heard him say. "Tell her not to worry about anything, either. She'll need time to grieve, and we'd like to pay for it all."

Jessica's fists clenched. Lacey's mother shuffled down the hallway without a backward look.

Jessica rose to Caleb's touch. He pulled her to her feet and she went into his embrace as if pulled by a vacuum. After a few minutes she felt Caleb guiding her to a chair and she sank down and curled up against the vinyl. She sat like that a long time, Caleb sitting beside her.

Later, Jessica left the hospital and drove aimlessly, leaving Caleb to wrap up details. On the seat beside her was a birth announcement that read "Baby Girl Bordelon." It was stamped with the baby's hand and footprints and carried the birth information. A woman in business clothes had delivered the announcement in an envelope to Lacey's room, but Lacey's mother had never come back and after a while Jessica walked in and took the packet from the empty bed. No one seemed to notice. There were a couple of Polaroid snapshots of the baby, blurred and dim, taken by one of the nurses, and a tiny bracelet with pink beads strung on elastic. The letters spelled BABY- GIRL.

When she stopped driving, she was at an over-look on the Louisiana side of the river. On the other side Natchez glowed in the light just before sundown. She parked the Subaru and walked along a paved trail along the riverbank. The water was twenty feet below her, but she was surprised at the size of the waves out in the current, as fast as whitewater. The river was about a half-mile wide, and downstream she could see the navigation lights on the river bridge and a few car headlights crossing the bridge high above the water. The water was muddy, and it swirled and surged and rippled as it raced toward New Orleans. Logs bobbed in the current, surfacing and submerging like alliga-tors, and garbage and brown foam and other flotsam spun in the eddies. The river was powerful and im-pressive, ugly and menacing. Jessica couldn't see the beauty or majesty that Mark Twain had seen in that water. I could step into that water and they wouldn't find my body for fifty miles, she thought. Maybe not even until New Orleans, if ever. It would be quick. She thought about it a long time, but then the light changed, bathing her in an orange glow and transforming Natchez across from her. Behind her, the sun had dipped below the cloud cover and fell into Louisiana, igniting multi-hued clouds and shooting sunbeams through their canyons, casting the bridge and the Mississippi shore with an otherworldly light. The colors stopped her from walking into the water.

Caleb lay down after *The Tonight Show*, his legs and back aching from too many hours on a dozer, and stared out the window at the pine trees, listening to the creak of branches rubbing against one another. He was too restless to sleep, and after a while he roamed through the house, picking up magazines and books and dropping them after reading a page or two and not being able to remember what he had just read. He picked up things that Jessica had handled and turned them over in his hands, as if a hairbrush or a watering can might give him the reason for her leaving, or show him how to get her back.

The wolves were skittish, wilded since Jessica left. When they finally came to him they stood off and bristled at his voice. Max slinked in and out of trees, looking dangerous as he passed from light into shadow, and Lulu braced her legs and held her head low to the ground, focusing on Caleb's movements like he was a deer to be stalked.

Caleb crouched in the dark and waited. He wished he had a cigarette, the craving sudden like the ghost pain of a lost limb. He followed Max with his eyes and tried not to tense when the wolf disappeared. Lulu crept toward him in increments, and he felt a surge of relief when she switched her tail and dropped her ears. He whispered to her in a soft voice, drawing her closer. Once he got the harness on her she waited by the gate. Max came around and submitted, bargaining human touch for a walk in the deeper woods. Caleb buckled the harness and led the wolves into the night. They ghosted around him like flowing water.

Caleb thought of Hubert earlier that afternoon, the dissipation through the set of his shoulders, the shuffle of his walk, the dead look in his eyes. Sitting in a chair with a roomful of cancer patients had to do that to a person, watching the medicine drip into each other's IVs, measuring the weight and hair loss over the past week. Hubert would be the last person in the world to accept sympathy, not that that was what Caleb felt. Would he miss Hubert when he died? He wondered what sort of hole would be left in the world. He thought, sometimes, that the place Hubert occupied in his life was just a shelf to place his anger.

After she died, the buffer his mother had provided was gone and Hubert and Caleb skirted one another like a snake coiled in the trail. Hubert practically moved out of the house and lived with his cattle, and when Hubert and Caleb were together the evenings were marked by long silences. Caleb spent hours in his room, taking apart small engines that he had salvaged from junkyards and listening to AM radio stations from Dallas, Houston, New Orleans, and St. Louis. Late at night, after he was supposed to be asleep, Caleb would crawl through his window and walk the woods and stare at the night sky and wonder about death and illness and Heaven and Hell and Jesus. He wondered about the life that he had with Hubert and compared it to the lives of the boys he knew in school and at church, boys who went hunting and fishing with their fathers, who played sports and whose fathers sat in the stands, cheering, boys who were confused by their fathers and who sometimes were angry with their fathers and who were certainly not friends with their fathers, but who at the same time knew their fathers and knew where they stood with them.

Many of those nights, Caleb crouched at the edge of the pasture and watched Hubert's truck make long slow circuits of his cattle, watched him park and sit in the cab and counted the match-flares as he smoked. Then Caleb would go through the woods and walk the bluffs above Black Creek, walking by sense other than sight. He found tall skinny saplings and shinnied high up the trunks, until the tree trembled beneath his weight and the slightest lean lowered him to the ground, where he released the tree and listened to it spring back into the sky and stood under the sprin- kling of leaves. He practiced walking silently, and he surprised animals bedded down for the night. Deer and bobcat exploded at his feet, stopping his heart, but he would slowly recover as they bounded away into the deeper shadows. He sat by the river where the current flowed over a gravel shoal and listened to the water sounds, the slap of beaver tails and sometimes the grunt of an alligator. He watched the ripple of snakes and muskrat swimming upstream. Sedimentary rocks and logs and tree roots were outlined in white foam and the clear smooth surface of the water became a deeper part of the night. Everywhere the rich smell of rotting logs and leaves, dirt, methane, animal musk, pine trees, and water. The soft whisper of hunting owls gliding overhead, tree-frogs ratcheting, the call of whip-or-wills and night hawk screams, the groan of trucks out on the highway, which couldn't be heard during the day but whose sound carried better at night. Caleb's nights.

Walking with the wolves, Caleb captured some- thing of the pleasure he had felt as a teenager, breaking rules, alive and awake while the rest of the world slept. He paid attention to what the wolves paid attention to. A frozen and alert Max would point out the movement of an animal a hundred yards away. Lulu's bristling nose held high in the air would prompt Caleb to identify wood smoke and shifting wind patterns. The wolves' ability to move silently heightened Caleb's frustration over his own awkwardness as he stumbled through the woods at night, trying to match their grace and fluidity. The only thing that would have enhanced those nights, Caleb thought, over and over, would have been to have Jessica.

"Look at that," Hubert said. He stared out the passenger window of the pickup at five coyotes that had broken from the tree line and were loping single-file across a pasture.

Caleb glanced out the window and caught the coyotes before they disappeared into tall grass, but it was difficult to look past Hubert. His skin was taut and pale and he wore a greasy John Deere cap to cover his lost hair. His body seemed to disappear inside his khaki work pants and long sleeve shirt rolled up to the elbows. He'd surprised Caleb that morning by calling and asking him to drive him to the feed store.

"'Bout the only good thing I can say for your wolves is the coyotes don't bother my cattle," Hubert continued. "This country's still stinking with them." Hubert hung his arm out the window and waved at the coyotes as they disappeared into the tree line. "Take it all," he said. "You can have the whole damn country now that I'm leaving."

Caleb thumbed the snapshot of his father that he kept in his shirt pocket.

"I was watching a program the other night on evolution," Hubert said. "What do you think about all of that?"

It was like hearing his father had cheated on his mother, or that he was planning to vote Democrat. "I don't know," Caleb said, looking over at him. Hubert still stared out the window. "You mean do I believe it?"

"I figure you must believe it. You don't believe what your mother and the Bible taught you all your life."

"Evolution has nothing to do with not going to church."

Hubert spat out the window. "You take the Bible and what I've always been taught. It says the world was created in six days. Six days. Spoken into existence. Daylight, stars and moon, dry land, plants, trees, birds, animals. Man and woman. My calculations show the world to be about ten thousand years old, but you got these scientists saying this here is sixty million years old, that there is eighty million years old."

"Did you add up all those genealogies in Genesis? Methusalah and what-not? They used to tell us 6,000 in Sunday school."

"I wonder how they do that. How do you pull a hundred million years out of a hat?"

"They got dating techniques," Caleb said. "Something to do with radiation, geological conditions. Erosion and stuff like that."

Hubert grunted, dismissing science. "But a million years. Can you even imagine a million years?"

"No."

"It's infinity is what it is. The preacher says God goes on forever and ever. He's been around forever, and after we're all dead and gone, we'll either end up in heaven singing praises forever, or we'll be in torment forever. Either way, it's infinity."

Caleb couldn't imagine his father in heaven, singing all day long. As a kid Caleb had never seen Hubert's mouth move during song service.

"Now you take me," Hubert said. "I've been on this earth for sixty-six years. In a lot of ways, that's a long,

long time. Right now it feels pretty short. But to you, sixty-six probably seems like forever."

"Not really."

"A million years. A hundred million years." Hubert shook his head. "I wish they'd never told us smoking causes cancer. Now I can't not think of myself as a sinner."

"I thought we were all sinners. 'We've all fallen short of the glory of God.'"

"We have," Hubert said. "And I'll have to answer when I meet God. I've destroyed his temple."

Caleb looked over at Hubert, but Hubert wouldn't meet his eyes.

"What do you think you'll say?" Caleb asked.

"Say?"

"How will you answer God when he asks you . . . . What do you think you'll say?"

"I meant pay up, not 'answer'. You don't answer God. You don't ask questions. There's nothing about your life you can explain or justify to Him. He knows all the answers. Job tried to question God, and when God got started talking, Job said 'Thank you sir. I'll just shut up and listen now.' You just wait for God to tell you what He thinks about the way you lived your life, and then you take what's coming to you."

They drove on for a while. Caleb counted the new houses that'd been built over the past few years. Town was steadily moving closer to home.

"I didn't think so much when I smoked," Hubert said. "I just worked and smoked and everything seemed a lot simpler."

"Did it?"

"Yeah, it did. I framed out the house where you grew up in three days—me and a helper—and that was humping it too. We used hand saws and hammer and nails. We didn't have power for circular-saws or nail guns back then. Daylight to dark, a can of potted meat and crackers and a smoke for lunch, then back at it. That was the best I could do, and everything fell right into place. But you take God *speaking* the *world* into existence in six days. I don't care if he did have the Son and the Holy Ghost helping Him. That was flat-out humping it. I have almost as much trouble seeing the world created in six days as I do a hundred million. I can't get a handle on either figure."

"I've heard some people say that the six days in *Genesis* were more like geological periods. Ice ages. Inland seas."

Hubert shook his head. "You believed that asshole in the White House wasn't a Muslim, either. You'll be-lieve about any shit they try to sell you, sometimes."

I believed your shit for years, Caleb thought.

Hubert took some papers and tobacco out of his shirt pocket and focused on rolling a cigarette. The paper rattled in the breeze from the window, so he rolled his side halfway and crouched over his work. He gave Caleb a look, and Caleb rolled up his window. After a couple of tries, his hands shaking and tobacco flakes flying off the paper, he crumbled up the mess and tossed it out.

"I don't know," Hubert said. The more I've been twisting it around and thinking about it, I guess I'd just as soon believe He did it in six days. It's all faith anyway, and at least with six days you've got some-thing solid in a God."

"I guess."

Hubert looked at Caleb. "You don't know what you believe anymore, do you?"

Caleb shook his head.

"I know you don't believe in what the church has taught you all these years."

"I'm leaning toward an agnostic, I guess."

"Jessica too?"

"I don't know what she thinks anymore. She's pretty mad at God right now."

"You think that bothers Him?"

Caleb shrugged his shoulders.

"You mad at God too?" Hubert asked.

"I guess I'm mad about a lot of things."

"Cry me a river."

Caleb flipped on the blinker and slowed to turn off the highway. After the turn he let the truck coast to a stop.

"You know what?" Caleb asked. "If I did believe in God, I'd be pretty pissed he gave me you for a father."

Hubert glared at Caleb, but he couldn't hold his son's stare and he turned back to his window. After a minute Caleb shifted down and let out the clutch and kept going. All the way to the feed store he replayed the conversation in his head.

When they got there Hubert opened his door and eased himself to the ground, then he shut the door and leaned in the window. "You'd best wait outside," he said. "These people don't care for wolf-loving liberals."

Caleb shrugged and nodded. There wasn't a single pickup in the parking lot without a rebel license plate or a full gun-rack, except his.

Hubert turned toward the steps leading up to the front of the store, but stopped and leaned in the window again. "I don't reckon God owes anybody any apologies," he said. "Me or you either one."

Jessica finished touching up the sculpture and drove back to her house. Her tank top was sweat-soaked and the air conditioning on the Subaru had stopped working. The dark vinyl seats burned her skin when she opened the car. She passed Tip's Bar, another old house converted into a business where college students liked mixing with locals. She pulled into the parking lot on a whim.

On the outside, Tip's looked like a meth house, but inside dark paneled walls covered with old concert posters, dart boards, and neon beer lights made for a good place for early drinkers to spend the afternoon. The bar was fronted by old toilets with padded lids fastened down for bar stools. Part of Tip's appeal was that it looked dangerous. The house had been partially gutted to make the inside roomier for dancing and pool tables.

Jessica sat down at one of the barstools and ordered a beer. The place wasn't crowded yet. The beer was cold and Tip had the thermostat turned down low. Jessica had always liked Tip's. It reminded her of a place in Pascagoula, where she had met Annie just after high school and the bartender just nodded at her fake ID. Jessica pulled out her pen and pad and doodled while she drank her beer. It was as good a defense against men inviting her into a conversation as a book, which wouldn't have felt right at Tip's. After a while Tip came over and asked if she wanted another drink and she nodded.

"Grocery list?" Tip asked. He looked like a stereotype, a character out of somewhere between *Deliverance* and *The Walking Dead*, but Jessica knew that he still took morning classes at the university and he had written some of the few letters to the editor supporting Caleb's op-ed pieces. Jessica smiled at him in appreciation, though he wouldn't know why.

"Just thinking."

"Don't go thinking too much," Tip said. "It's bad for the bar business."

"I was just thinking about being eighteen," Jessica said. "A long time ago."

"It's hard not to when you hit a certain age." He smiled and looked like he was thinking about it himself. "That kind of thinking is good for the bar business," he said. "This one's on the house." He set the beer down and moved to wait on a couple of guys who'd walked in.

Jessica couldn't remember the name of the bar in Pascagoula. She had graduated high school and just started out at the shipyards as a welder's helper, courtesy of her father's pull with the union. She spent the day stretching cords, fetching welding rods, tacking plate, getting cursed at, hit on, and cleaning up. She worked the three to eleven shift, the most unpopular shift— except for people who wanted to have affairs— since it took away anything like a normal social life. There was nothing for Jessica to do after work but go home and try to be quiet while her parents slept, so she started going to the bars that lined the beaches along the Mississippi Sound, swampland drained and sprinkled with sand to manufacture a beach. Bars stayed open till 2 a.m. and then parties drifted out onto the sand or back to apartments. Most nights Jessica was satisfied to go home after a couple of beers, mainly having wanted to wait for her parents to go to bed.

One of the regulars was a guy named Vann. He worked the same shift at the shipyard but on a different crew, and Jessica would see him from night to night. Early twenties, Brad Pitt handsome, Vann had gone to Alaska after high school and stayed long enough to marry Annie, an Anchorage girl a couple of years older than Jessica, pretty and a little helpless, like the girl in the first *Terminator*. They'd come south for the winter to live with Vann's parents and save up some money for another try at the big money construction jobs in Alaska once the weather broke in the spring. Evenings, Annie waited outside the shipyard for Vann to get off, since they only had a 70s model crew-cab Ford with a camper shell on the bed. Vann made her keep a pistol with her, but Annie had confided to Jessica that she kept it unloaded. After work they usually wound up at the bar, especially after Jessica met Annie and they hit it off.

Jessica had never really had a girlfriend. In high school she'd been too shy or considered too weird—messing around with tools in her father's workshop and knowing how to weld made her gay, and once she started at the shipyard, most of the women were hard drinking, hard fighting roughnecks, or women beaten down by the long hours and the demands of husbands and ex-husbands and children—neither type had time for a teenager. Annie sparked something in Jessica, having come from an exotic place where snow fell and the wilderness was wide open and expansive, not choked off by canals and marshes and thick forests and swamps. Annie hated Mississippi—the weather, the people, the muddy Sound, Vann's parents, her job as a bank teller.

"Those people stretch words like they're rubber bands," she'd said. They were sitting on the beach at two a.m., in front of a fire with a fine mist coming down.

"There're animals on the walls," she said. "I mean I grew up in Alaska for god's sake. I get trophy heads, but his parents' house is morbid." She took a cigarette from a pack someone had left on a beach towel and lit it. As she exhaled, her face relaxed for the first time since Jessica had met her. "I can see the point of having one of every-thing," she said. "A deer, a moose, an elk. But they've got eight deer. It's like Hemingway went hunting."

Jessica laughed about it and then Annie got serious. She took out one of the cigarettes and handed it to her. Jessica shook her head but she pressed it. "Vann'll get mad when he smells the smoke on me. Let me tell him it was you."

"He knows I don't smoke."

"Tell him you started."

Annie talked about Anchorage booming with oil and new construction. In the summers, the sun barely set. There were a few short hours that were more heavy twilight than full dark, and she and Vann hiked in the mountains crowding Anchorage against the Cook Inlet until midnight or 1 a.m. The stories about the occasional earthquake, moose walking through neighborhoods, black bears in the garbage and the occasional Brown bear glimpsed in the Glen Alps above town sparked Jessica's longing to leave Mississippi and go somewhere else. She'd long dreamed of getting out, and anywhere West or North had long fascinated her. She'd even taken French in high school just to join the French club and go on the spring break trip to Quebec. Two years of French for one day of snow-skiing in Canada.

All through the fall and winter and early spring after high school Jessica saved money by living at home and hanging out with Vann and Annie after work. After the bars Vann usually fell asleep on the couch in the apartment, or if they were at a bonfire on the beach, he'd just roll up in a blanket. He went fishing and hunting two or three times a week, often camping out with his buddies from work or high school, and he liked having Jessica with Annie to keep her occupied. Annie liked to sit in front of a fire on the beach on cool evenings, nursing a beer and talking to Jessica. Most of what Jessica knew about sex she'd learned from Annie, much more that what her mother had ever taught her. When Annie mentioned making the drive back to Anchorage with her and Vann in May, it didn't take much for Jessica to sign onto the trip. She would pay a third of the gas and food, and once they got to Anchorage and Vann and Annie found a place, Jessica could rent Annie's old room from her parents. There would be plenty of jobs in the summer, especially after the fishing boats started running and the canneries opened. Welders' helpers were always in work. It was the chance of a lifetime.

They left in early May, late enough that the Mississippi spring had turned to summer, and about as early as they could expect the Alaskan Highway to be drivable. Annie rode in the middle, her feet propped on the transmission hump in the floorboard. Jessica stared out the passenger window and watched time move backward, summer turning to spring and then late winter. The crew cab was made up into a bed, a thin foam mat on top of boxes of books and clothes. The camper shell was packed full of Vann's guns and camping gear and furniture. As soon as Vann got behind the wheel of the pickup he became a long distance truck driver bent on racking up mileage, every move dictated by the road atlas he kept in his lap. They ate sandwiches and drank cokes from the cooler while driving and he accused Annie of excessive whining. He only exited the interstate for gas and if anyone had to pee it was just tough luck. He worried about the weather and shushed them whenever they joked about the trucker static on the CB that was mounted to the dash above Annie's knees.

As soon as they crossed the South Dakota state line, the skies passed from a monotonous gray to a world of white that only existed a hundred yards beyond the windshield. When night fell, the lanes became indistinguishable from the snowdrifts stretching beyond the headlights.

Annie worked on Vann to stop at Mt. Rushmore the next day. "Just long enough to buy a postcard and snap a couple of pictures. The Black Hills are supposed to be beautiful with snow."

"You know how far off the interstate we'll have to drive?" he asked. He bent over the steering wheel, concentrating on the sloppy roads.

"You're holding the map," she said. "Why don't you tell us?"

"We'll see."

"Seventy-five hundred miles," Annie said to Jessica. "Another hundred or so won't kill us."

"We'll see."

"You know what 'we'll see' means when your parents say it," Annie said to Jessica.

"No," Jessica said.

Vann shot a look at Jessica, then to Annie he said, "You're the one been crying about living in Mississippi." He set his mouth in a tight line.

They'd driven fourteen hours that day, or rather Vann had driven fourteen hours, all the way from Kansas City up along the edge of Iowa to South Dakota. The day before they'd started out in Mississippi. Both Annie and Jessica offered to help him drive, but he refused, saying, "I want to go the whole way, Mississippi to Alaska. I want to be able to say I made the drive solo."

"Are you having an adventure yet?" Annie whispered.

The only thing interesting had been watching the tension between Vann and Annie sprout like an angry color. Jessica shook her head at the question and said, "Not yet." The windshield wipers had iced over and the defroster couldn't keep up with the storm.

Vann stopped at a campground in South Dakota. The cab of the truck cooled with the motor off and their breath formed a fine white frost on the windows. Jessica opened the door, but a blast of wind blew it shut.

"I'll set up your tent," Vann said. "It can be tricky."

"I did it last night."

"We were in Missouri last night. Better enjoy the warm," he said. He buttoned his jacket and pulled on a pair of wool gloves with the fingertips cut out, then stepped out into the storm.

Annie climbed over the seat into the extended cab and made out their bed with blankets and sleeping bags. "Well," she said. She zipped Vann›s parka higher and shivered. Her blonde hair mashed flat under her earmuffs and her body disappeared inside the folds of the jacket. "Maybe Vann will let us run the heater tonight."

"Too much gas."

"You sound just like him," she said.

Jessica searched the pockets of her jacket for gloves.

"I'm sorry," Annie said. "Talking about the heater. Do you have thermals?"

Jessica patted her thigh. "Long johns, wool socks, a goose down jacket and a wool cap. I'll be okay."

"If it gets too bad knock on the window."

"That would ruin the adventure, wouldn't it?"

"It's been pretty boring if you ask me."

The driver's door opened and a swirl of snow followed Vann inside. He blew on his fingers and clapped his hands together. "Tent's all set up," he said. "I rolled out your sleeping bag."

"Did you put the ground cloth down?" Annie asked.

He gave her a look. "Now why would I not put down a ground cloth when she's going to be sleeping on fresh wet snow?"

"Just checking."

Vann turned to Jessica and explained the thermodynamics of camping in the snow with his eighth-grade science teacher voice: "The snow will actually work as insulation. You'll be warmer than us. That's a zero-degree bag." He took his jacket off and laid it across the steering wheel to dry. Annie gave Jessica a peck on the cheek and a guilty smile, and she stepped out into the slanting snow.

The bag was cold, but it warmed with her body and for an hour or two it was tolerable. The storm intensified during the night, and the walls of the tent puffed and strained and sucked in and out like an old man gasping for breath before it collapsed under the wind. Jessica lay under the weight and rubbed her feet together, hoping the canopy would act as a second blanket, but under the weight of the snow the canvas pressed around her and began to leak, driving a deep chill on whichever side she wasn't lying. Her boots were buried somewhere near her feet, and she inched out from underneath the weight of the tent and snow, sockfooted, with the bag draped around her shoulders. She tried the door of the pickup. Locked. She rapped and waited and rapped again, but they either couldn't hear her over the wind noise or chose not to. The only light in the campground was the shower house, so she made a dash for it. The ladies' room was locked, but the men's was open. The electric hand dryer ran exactly thirty seconds before shutting off each time, no matter how many times she pushed the button. She huddled under it and listened to the wind whip around the building and thought about how the pickup must be shaking. She imagined Vann and Annie together in the tiny bed inside the extended cab, and Vann, pausing, pressed into Annie, shaking his head no as Jessica knocked on the window.

Asshole.

A foot of snow covered everything in the morning. Annie met Jessica in the restroom and they smoked a couple of cigarettes before Annie brushed her teeth and washed her face. As they walked back to the truck with the sleeping bag draped over her shoulders, Jessica didn't feel as cold as she thought it should be. The morning was bright and the light hurt her eyes. She remembered her sunglasses in the glove compartment. Vann stood beside the mound of snow over the collapsed tent, his hands in his jacket pockets. He looked up at the sound of crunching snow under Annie's boots and smiled. "I thought I was going to have to dig you out," he said.

"Wishful thinking," Jessica said.

Later that afternoon in Wyoming, they either caught up to the storm from the night before or drove into a new one. Jessica loved the way the snow blanked out the world, the way the flakes curved through the headlights and into the windshield, the way the snow mounded on trees and buildings and parked cars, softening the edges. In Mississippi a half inch shut down schools and businesses and turned the streets into a demolition derby.

Annie and Vann argued about a motel for the night. Annie pushed for Sheridan in Wyoming. She'd commandeered the road atlas and held onto it. Vann wanted to make Montana and a rest stop he'd seen on the map. Annie wasn't having it, and Vann started in on her about money and how she'd spent the last year complaining about missing her parents and ragging on Mississippi.

Jessica couldn't imagine spending the night outside again, not with a wet tent and sleeping bag, but she kept out of it.

"Half of a cheap room isn't going to kill any of us. Just find a place," Annie said. "Okay? That's all I've got to say to you tonight."

With the snow, the dark wasn't as dark as it should have been. It was too quiet in the truck, and Jessica wished the snow was louder, like a thunderstorm pounding the roof and roaring under the wheel wells, drowning out everything. She concentrated on the slap of the windshield wipers and thought about how good a warm bath would feel.

"Non-smoking," Vann said. "You two can go outside if you need to support your habit."

The room was a dark-paneled cube with two twin beds and a wall heater, but once the pizza came and the room warmed, everyone was in a better mood. Vann propped against the headboard of the bed next to the bathroom, closest to the TV. He tuned into a basketball game with the sound all the way off and wrote a few notes in his travel log, then studied the *Mileposts*.

Annie took a shower and came out in fresh teal long johns and one of Vann's long flannel shirts. She sat on the bed next to Vann and brushed her hair. "You should try the bath," she said to Jessica. "It's wonderful."

Vann put down his magazine and pulled Annie closer. She curled into him and his hand moved down the back of her thigh. She giggled and pulled away from him, looking over her shoulder at Jessica, who carried her things into the bathroom and shut the door. She started the bath water and sat on the toilet and stared at the door.

When the tub was full she shut the water off. Outside the bed creaked and Annie giggled; Jessica wished Vann would turn the sound up on the TV. Water dripped from the faucet and outside the wind pelted snow against the frosted window. She opened the cold valve to a trickle, hoping it would cover their lovemaking. Water gurgled though the overflow drain just below the faucet and Jessica closed her eyes and listened.

She must have slept—she wasn't sure, but when she opened her eyes the room had a different energy. The sounds from the other side of the door had changed. They were talking, but it wasn't love talk anymore. Vann's voice got louder and the bed creaked. A sound like a hand clap. Annie crying. Then she was at the door to the bathroom, knocking and rattling the locked door.

"Let me in," she said. Her voice was choked, farther away than the thin door that separated them.

Jessica opened the door. Annie stood there in her thermal top and panties. Her hand covered her nose and blood leaked past her fingers and dribbled down her chin. She pushed past Jessica and in the same motion pushed her out into the motel room and slammed the door. A trail of bright blood drops led to Annie's bed, where Vann sat against the headboard, shirtless, with a sheet pulled to his waist. The open *Mileposts* lay beside him and he looked up at Jessica, his finger marking his spot. She went to her bed and sat down.

"What happened?"

"Nosebleed," he said, and looked down at his magazine. "She gets them a lot."

"Why is she so upset then?"

"I don't know," Vann said. "Maybe she's embarrassed." He turned a page and looked at her. "It's a nosebleed. Don't make too much out of it."

Jessica walked back to the bathroom door and knocked. Water splashed in the sink. "Annie?"

"Not now," she said.

"Annie. Do you need some help?"

"No."

Jessica turned the knob. Annie stood in front of the mirror holding a stained washcloth to her face. Jessica shut the door and went to her and held her by the shoulders. She turned her face away. The water spinning down the drain was tinged red. Jessica reached for another washcloth and wet it.

"I think it's stopped now," she said.

Jessica turned Annie's face until she was looking at her and took the cloth away. Her nose and cheek had begun to swell and the bruise was beginning to darken her face. Jessica dabbed at a trace of blood with the new cloth.

"What happened? She whispered."

Annie shook her head and took the cloth.

"Here, sit down," Jessica said, guiding her.

Annie dropped the toilet seat and sat. Jessica covered her legs with a clean towel and kneeled beside her.

"You don't have to go back out there."

"Yes I do."

"No, you don't."

Annie shook her head again. "You don't understand."

"We can take the bus in the morning," Jessica whispered. "I've got a credit card."

Annie handed her the cloth and pointed at the sink. Jessica stood and rinsed it out and kneeled beside her again.

"Okay. When we get to your parent's house you can kick him out. Your mom and dad won't put up with this if they know."

Annie leaned forward with her hands on her knees, kneading the washcloth between her fingers. She stared at the door, her eyes empty, and Jessica thought for a moment that she was considering life without Vann. Jessica kneeled beside her.

"I'll get a job when we get there. You can go to school."

Annie looked at her and sighed, and then she smiled. "You're so noble." She stood up, dropping the towel that covered her legs. She stepped in front of the mirror and cleaned the tears from her face. She rewet the cloth and held it to her cheek. "I need a little while with him," she said. "Your bath's probably cold, but there should be more hot water." She gave Jessica a pat on the cheek and started for the door.

"Wait a second," Jessica said.

"What?" She turned, annoyed.

"Never mind."

"I'm sorry you saw us like this," Annie said. "It's not like this. Really. We have a lot of good times."

"Okay," Jessica said. She watched her go. She closed the door behind her. She pulled the plug on the bathtub and watched the water drain, then filled it again with scalding water. She sat on the toilet and waited for the water to cool. The motel room quieted and the storm even seemed to die down for a while. Drops fell from the faucet into the water, creating tiny ripples. When Jessica was sure that Vann and Annie were asleep, she opened the bathroom door. The room was dark except for the TV, which was turned to some sort of infomercial —three women sitting around a pile of makeup on a coffee table. Vann was still propped against the headboard and Annie lay beside him, her head on his chest and her eyes closed. Her breathing showed her to be asleep. Vann focused on the TV as he idly stroked her hair.

"Better get a good night's sleep," he said. "We've got a long day tomorrow. Got to make up for today. Should make Canada."

Jessica looked through her bag and ignored him, but when she looked up Vann was staring at her. Jessica pulled back the covers and started to get in, but instead walked across the room to where her boots were drying on a chair in front of the wall heater. They were warm on the outside, still damp on the inside. She turned them. The leather was stiff.

"They getting dry?" Vann asked.

"Yeah. I think I'll need something better when we get to Anchorage, though."

"You just need some snow-seal. Or a good coat of oil."

"Yeah." Jessica walked over to the TV and turned it off. The room went dark.

"Hey!"

"I can't sleep with the TV on," Jessica said.

He didn't say anything so she crawled into bed and pulled the covers up to her chin. The sheets were cold and the wind outside had picked up again. It reminded her of sleeping in the attic of her grandmother's house in a rainstorm, the wind blowing and rain pelting the tin roof. She knew that she wouldn't fall asleep anytime soon.

They drove for days, hundreds of miles of unpaved roads tracing the shoulders of river valleys and crossing mountain passes. Vistas of plains sparkled as the sun glinted off the melting snow and newly released water. The forests were thick fir and spruce, and moose grazed on the right of way. Occasionally a silver fox crossed the road, and once at an overlook Vann pointed out a pack of wolves a half mile away, loping through a river valley. Rivers and creeks overflowed their banks with a silvery silt-laden snow melt. They drove through little villages of log cabins lined by rickety fences and yards littered with logging trucks and sidelined snowmobiles, rusting parts grown up in weeds, heating oil drums, and wildflowers. Wolfish dogs roamed free or were chained and they clamored at the passing truck. When they stopped for gas the stations were close and dark inside, stuffed with tools and clothing and almost everything a person might need to survive a closed-in winter, except food, where the shelves were picked over and waiting resupply. Annie and Jessica drew long, appreciative stares everywhere they went, and Vann grew grumpier the further north they drove. Annie grew more distant toward Jessica and doubled-down on Vann. Vann talked about some friends he knew who Jessica might be able to split rent with, and she understood that staying with Annie's parents was no longer an option. She settled back and made the best of the drive, determined to open herself up to this new land and let whatever was going to happen, happen.

Caleb stopped where the county road joined the four lane and watched the steady stream of cars marked by their headlights. DeSoto was a few miles north. Turn left and he could be at the Mississippi Sound in Biloxi in forty-five minutes. A tractor-trailer whished past, rocking Caleb's pickup. There was nowhere he wanted or needed to go. There was the new mall, which he had only been in once or twice with Jessica. The movie theatre, but he had no idea what might be playing. The bars would be full of college kids, or worse, people he'd interviewed at some point. He hated the idea of going anywhere alone. Jessica would recognize his truck if he drove past her house. Their phone calls had become infrequent and awkward.

He ended up at the Po-Boy Express, a chrome and plastic diner that made New Orleans style sandwiches. He had delivered for them in college, but there was a new owner and he didn't know anyone there. He went inside and ordered a muffuletta and fries from a girl with a pierced navel, and he took a seat by the window so he could stare out at the traffic. The walls were lined with sports memorabilia from the university, framed and signed jerseys, old schedules, photos. The radio in the kitchen was tuned to the college station playing music that sounded like Bob Dylan but wasn't.

From the first day Jessica had taken to the wolves and they had taken to her like they came from the same litter. That first night she'd walked up to the pen and kneeled before them and waited patiently for the wolves to accept her. Both wolves had sniffed her over after the initial skittishness, then licked her face in their show of social submission.

"That seemed to go okay," Jessica had said.

They walked down to the river, following Max and Lulu on their leads. It felt natural to Caleb. They stood on the bank and watched the wolves explore the new concept of moving water.

The waitress brought Caleb's sandwich to him with a cup of coffee. He tried not to stare at her navel but couldn't help it. The sandwich was the size of a dinner-plate, round bread fried in olive oil, with deli meat, cheese, and olive salad inside. The girl left the table without saying anything and Caleb looked up, relieved, just in time to see Jessica pulling away from the drive-thru window and drive past him before turning onto the street. A young guy was sitting in the passenger seat, one of the graduate students from her program, and he and Jessica had been laughing about something. Caleb didn't think that she had seen him.

It was after midnight when Caleb got out of bed and dressed. The night was a little cooler than usual, a suggestion of fall that was still too far off. He slept better in the cold, but he had lain awake for what seemed like forever, replaying the image of Jessica pulling out of the drive-thru, the laughter on her face, the way she failed to see him sitting at an orange booth in the fluorescent glare of the restaurant. He had spent the evening moping, sipping from a six pack and driving back roads.

He walked downstairs to the kitchen and thought about the last beer in the refrigerator. He caught his reflection in the window above the sink. His hair was getting long, falling below his collar, though his scalp showed through the thinning hair on the top of his head. He picked his Texas Rangers ball cap and covered it up. With the hat on his face looked younger, his hair fuller. He didn't have any expression that he could name. Tight lipped and serious. He tried a smile, but stretching his mouth that way didn't look natural.

It seemed like such a long time since Jessica had left him, even though it was less than a month. When she had been there, she liked to stay up late, watch Jimmy Fallon, and then when the one station signed off and the other only offered Brother Quitman, they would go out and walk with the wolves if the weather was good. Sometimes Jessica told him about Alaska, about seeing the pipeline. The tundra felt so big, stretching away to where the mountains seemed to rise out of flat ground like an island, white against the brown grassy plain. The pipeline staggered across the plain, mile after mile, elevated above the frozen ground, wrapped in a heated jacket to keep the oil flowing even in the coldest winter. Caleb had been surprised to hear that the pipeline wasn't welded together in straight, rigid sections. There were soft joints between each section so the pipeline could float above the expansion and contraction of the tundra that came with each cycle of freeze and thaw. The welders who'd made those joints, she'd said, were craftsmen, some of the best welders in the world. Caleb imagined the pipeline crawling across Alaska like a long thin snake with oil flowing through it like blood through a vein. She'd bought the Subaru in Anchorage, used, and one day she'd parked on a rise of ground overlooking a stretch of pipeline. Through her binoculars she'd watched a pack of wolves worry a moose across the tundra. She said that from a distance it looked more like the swirling dance of ballerinas imitating a snowstorm, rather than an intricate struggle between life and death. They never got the moose, as far as she could tell, but the way they dashed in and out, ripping at its flanks, avoiding its hooves and sweeping antlers, had been beautiful.

Caleb had a picture of her, standing underneath the pipeline with the landscape blurring in the distance. Jessica stood with her hands over her head so that it looked like she was holding the section of pipe above her. Her hair was long and windblown, and she was laughing. He had wondered who had taken the picture of her before, wishfully hoping that it must be some stranger stopped at the same roadside pullout. But now he had an image in his mind of Jessica with another man, even though she'd always been alone in every picture he had seen. Thinking about it made a new knot in his stomach, and he went to the refrigerator for the last beer and stood in front of the window to drink it.

He had bought the wolves because of Alaska, even though he knew it was a fool's move, like the guy who thought he could walk out of the stands at the Superdome at halftime and kick a twenty-five-yard field goal for a thousand dollars. Wolves in Mississippi had nothing to do with Alaska, especially the part of it that Jessica had never shared with him—the full truth of Alaska. But he also knew that before Jessica his life had been nothing more than one day of work followed by another, sunrise followed by sunset, with little to nothing in between.

He had found the wolves on the way to a big used equipment and livestock sale in Diboll, Texas. It was there that he first saw the sign outside a country gas station advertising wolf pups. He left after Jessica went to bed and drove most of the night pulling a low-boy trailer and homing in on WBAP 820 out of Dallas. After the Rangers baseball game and a call-in sports show, the station played country music and gave weather reports for truck drivers. The call-in show had been about the border wall with Mexico and the government taking land away from the ranchers and homeowners along the Rio Grande. The callers couldn't decide who they hated more—the Mexicans coming across the border or the government for taking their land. The weather reports reminded Caleb of the nights after his mother died, putting himself to sleep listening to weather from across the country, imagining life beyond Mississippi. That night there were

thunderstorms on I-75 between Knoxville and Chat-
tanooga, high winds across Kansas and Nebraska, I-10
west of Houston was under construction. The station
grew stronger throughout the early morning. Just before sunrise he stopped for gas and coffee. The store
had two pumps and a pre-fab metal transmission shop
off to one side. Caleb studied the sign while he waited
for the pump to click off.

Inside, he browsed through a display of DVDs. He
filled a Styrofoam cup with coffee and wandered to
the counter where a girl about fifteen wrapped sausage biscuits in cellophane. Caleb bought a couple and
asked about the wolves. "We got a bunch," she said.
"But you'll have to see Mike about that. He's the only
one can get around them bastards."

Mike wasn't going to be there until that afternoon,
so Caleb went on to the sale and picked up a used Caterpillar D-7 bulldozer for a reasonable price. It needed
some work.

After he got the Cat loaded onto the flatbed, he
wandered around the sale barn. Hubert had brought
him here years before. He attributed his success to
Texas bulls, claiming they were tougher than anything
bred in Mississippi. Pickups pulling livestock trailers
full of cattle, goats, sheep, and hogs moved around
the yard, getting in position to load or unload at
the maze of corrals covering a couple of acres. The
livestock men wore wide-brimmed hats and cowboy
boots. Caleb walked through the holding pens, looking
at bulls. Despite being raised around cattle all his life,
Caleb had always hated stepping in cow shit. Hubert
had never minded. By the end of the day his boots
were crusted over and he always forgot to take them
off at the door. The only regret his mother ever had

about marrying Hubert, Caleb once overheard her tell another woman at church, was that he always smelled like his work and wore it home at the end of the day.

Some men drove a load of Hereford calves down a trailer ramp and into a holding pen. A fine mist of rain fell. The calves stumbled around, finding their legs like tourists on Bourbon Street. One of the calves trotted around the pen licking the fence posts. The rest huddled over some stale hay spotted with their own shit that one of the men threw down from the truck.

To Caleb, cows were simple eating machines. The young bulls would try to hump each other for a while, even after they were castrated, but when they discovered food life slowed down. One day he had watched a herd stand huddled together through a hailstorm, the high wind and thunder turning the pasture into a glacier. They chewed at the ground, ignoring the marbles bouncing off their backs and didn't even look up until he broke the twine on a fresh round of hay.

Hubert had taught him how to castrate bulls when he was nine, and after punishing him for letting the cow die, he had taught Caleb how to properly palpate a birthing cow. The first time he stuck his skinny arm inside, his father said he didn't even need Vaseline. It was moist, so warm it seemed to burn his skin, the heat off the cow breaking Caleb into a sweat. Hubert told him how to find the head of the calf and turn it down, how to find the front legs of the calf and pull. He still hadn't been strong enough to pull it down himself and his father held his forearms to help. Caleb was sickened by the smell, then amazed at the awkward tangle of life that couldn't stand on its own for the first hour or so, but it didn't take long for the wonder to go out of it, and Caleb thought that was when journalism started looking good to him.

Caleb leaned on a fence to get out of people's way. A short Hispanic man worked a huge red Brahma with a cane and a mottled blue cur. The dog was a thing of beauty, moving the bull with nips at the hindquarters, dodging the kicking legs and sweeping horns. Caleb picked out the man's curse words, the only Spanish he remembered from the migrant workers Hubert had sometimes hired, reluctantly. They would sleep in the barn for the week or so they worked and Caleb would listen to them at night, listen to the way they talked and laughed. It sounded like the tinny music on the mariachi radio stations he picked up late at night when the AM came in clear across the Gulf of Mexico. At lunch Caleb would swap ham and cheese sandwiches for tamales. He'd sit in the cab of the truck and unwrap the corn husks and peel apart the tamale just to find the shiny black olive in the middle, an exotic fruit. The only olives Caleb had ever seen were tiny and green and stuffed with pimento, the kind served at church potlucks. It amazed him to think that these migrants had something so wonderful as an olive when they had little or nothing else.

The Brahma snorted and made a run at the man. The dog nipped at its hooves. As the man stepped aside, he broke his cane over the bull's head and punched it with the pointy end. The bull stopped on a dime and shook his heavy horns. The cur stood at attention, daring the bull.

The only joke Hubert knew was about the young bull and the old bull, standing in a pasture and eying a herd of cows on the other side of the fence. The young bull told the old one that he thought he might jump the fence and screw one of those cows. The old bull thought about that for a minute, and then said he was going to walk around the fence and screw all of them. Hubert would almost fall down laughing every time he told that, though Caleb got a whipping when Hubert overheard him tell the same joke to some boys at church. Caleb was never sure whether it was the language that angered Hubert, or just the fact that someone had the audacity to laugh in church. Probably both.

Hubert's life had been consumed by cattle, which meant Caleb's life had been consumed by cattle. Getting up at five every winter morning, hunching in the cab of the pickup waiting for the heater to warm up, making rounds on the cattle they had looked at seven hours before, the last thing before going to bed every night. Brucellosis and bangs disease, hay to rotate, shit on his boots, and the ever-present coyotes that Hubert always fumed about but that Caleb found to be one of his few sources of pleasure whenever he listened to them sing at night or saw four or five loping across the pasture at first light.

The auctioneer started in over the PA system, his voice ringing through the stockyard, announcing that the sale would start in twenty minutes. The man had his bull in a holding pen, ready to start it down the runway when his turn came. The cur flopped on the ground beside Caleb and bit at its stubby tail. A wind kicked up and the rain came harder, driving groups of men toward the sale barn. The Hispanic man climbed onto a metal gate and smacked the bull with his broken cane one last time, then pulled out a pack of cigarettes and lit one. He looked over at Caleb and offered the pack, but he shook his head no.

"Bueno perro," Caleb said. He bent down to pet the dog, but it bit harder at what was left of its tail.

"Yes, he's a good dog." The man slouched down against the rain and smoked his cigarette.

Caleb watched the silvery planks of the sale barn turn dark with the rain while he scratched the dog's back. Driving home, he met a convoy of pulpwood trucks sagging under full loads, heading toward the particleboard plant in Diboll or the paper mill in Tyler. The trucks were rusted and dented, wiring hanging loose under the frame, doors welded shut. Running on bald tires with no headlights and worn brakes, like it was a condition to enter the business. The pines grew right up to the edge of the highway, but the trees were little more than a windbreak. The clear cuts extended away from the highway and out of sight, mile after mile.

A mile past the store where he'd bought gas that morning, Caleb circled the truck and trailer in a big U-turn and went back. His back hurt from driving all night, and he felt gritty and he had the scent of cow manure in his nostrils. The girl from that morning was gone, replaced by a black woman frying chicken for the display counter. When she asked what he wanted, Caleb asked for Mike. The woman pointed toward the transmission shop. The garage was dark, but the sound of a pneumatic tool ran over a radio swap program. He went toward it, stepping around transmission housings, old tires, and piles of junk. The only light came from underneath an old Willys jeep parked over a mechanic's pit. When Caleb called out a guy stuck his head out, pushing up a drop cord light to see.

"I'm curious about the wolves." Caleb said.

The man crawled out from underneath the jeep and stood up. He pulled a dirty shop rag out of his back pocket and looked Caleb over as he wiped his hands. His mustache didn't meet his beard, leaving bare patches below the corners of his mouth. He wore dark blue coveralls with an outline of Texas in yellow on his back.

"You ain't from the state?"

"I saw your sign this morning. I been to the sale at Diboll." A calendar hung from an I-beam, a woman in a bikini straddling a shiny transmission like she was riding a horse.

Mike picked up a wrench and scratched his back, closing his eyes and going deep. "You didn't see no wolves at the sale, did you?" He sat on the fender of the Willys and lit a cigarette.

"Just the usual." Mike's index finger was missing a joint and Caleb wondered if it was the wolves.

"You sure you ain't with the state?"

"I'm sure."

Mike motioned for him to follow and they walked out the back of the shop and down a dirt road through some woods.

"Going to be a hot summer once the rains taper off," Mike said, then walked in silence. After a couple hundred yards they came to a low-slung, faded wood barn with a rusty tin roof.

The floor was cement, twenty chain link kennels running the length of both sides. The room was quiet except for the rustling of padded feet and the scrape of fur on metal. In the pen just opposite the door a wolf twice the size of the biggest German shepherd Caleb had ever seen stared at hin.

"I wouldn't try to pet anything," Mike said. "They'll take your hand off they don't know you."

Caleb went to his knees in front of the pen and watched the wolf's nose work. The wolf was dusty brown and its eyes didn't blink.

Mike walked down the row of kennels, calling each wolf by name, explaining the blood lines and which were related to one another. The wolves were all shades of grey, black, brown and white; none were as large as the first. The eyes were attentive, displaying something not far short of an imaginative intelligence that spooked Caleb a little.

"How many?" Caleb asked.

"Twenty two counting the pups."

"People buy these?"

"You'd be surprised. I had one guy near Waco bought a three-hundred acre horse farm, fenced it eight foot all around. He's got a whole pack now." MIke stopped in front of one pen and let a wolf lick his hand through the link. "I tried wolf-husky mixes. Quarter, half, three quarter, seven-eighths. They're too unpredictable in my book. Tend to kill things when you least expect it. Professional dog fighters liked them, but I don't tolerate cruelty. I go full blood now. At least you know what you got."

"Full blood is more dependable?"

Mike shrugged his shoulders. "You want dependable get a dog." He kneeled down and opened one of the gates for a dark gray with white feet. It spooked back from Caleb, but after a minute or two came to the door and licked Mike's ears.

"Maggie had a litter this spring. She's a real sweetheart. Here. Drop down and let her smell you."

Caleb went to his knees and offered the back of his hand. Maggie sniffed it, then took his hand in her mouth. The teeth were razors even though the touch was light.

"She likes you," Mike said. "She won't mouth just anybody."

"She lets go, don't she?"

"How much money you got?" Mike looked serious for a second before he laughed. He shook Maggie's mouth and she released Caleb's hand. "Come look at these pups, then I got to get back to work."

Caleb wiped his hand on his jeans while Mike closed the gate, then they went into a small room at the end of the barn. It was warm, not as well-lit as the main room. From the corner came whining and grunts and the sounds of tiny wolf bodies struggling over one another.

"I got two litters, separate blood, in case you're interested in breeding," Mike said. He opened a chicken wire pen and half a dozen furry footballs fell out. Caleb knelt and they swamped him, all sniffing, biting, peeing on the floor.

Mike went over to some shelves and rattled around. He filled the food bowls and topped off the water trough, then he leaned against the counter and watched Caleb play for a few minutes.

"Well Mr. Curious. I'm fixing to yank the drive shaft out of that Willys. You want to talk money?"

"What do they eat?"

"Dry dog food, mostly. But you got to mix in some meat. A lot of meat. Liver is best. They ain't far enough domesticated to fully process grain."

The wolves' teeth pricked like being jabbed with an icepick. One grabbed Caleb by the coat sleeve and wouldn't let go. It just growled harder the more he tried to push it away. Beautiful animals.

"Okay," he said. "Let's talk money."

Later, Caleb and Mike each carried a wolf to the pickup, a male and a female from separate litters. Mike sold him a dog kennel and lined the bottom with an old blanket. Just as Caleb was about to leave, a school bus pulled up on the highway and the girl he'd talked to that morning got off. She slung a backpack and walked over to the truck.

"You found Mike," she said.

"What's your name?"

"Lulu." She swept a strand of hair out of her eyes.

"Okay if I name the female Lulu?"

"It's your wolf," she said.

Caleb saw she was pleased, though she tried not to show it. "What do you want to call the male?"

Lulu studied the two cubs for a minute. "How about Max? Max and Lulu."

"I like the sound of that," Caleb said. He climbed in the truck and pulled out, splashing through the mud puddles that dotted the gravel. The sky was getting dark and it looked like it would rain on the way home. The female cub soon fell asleep, but the male sat up and chewed on the edge of the kennel. Caleb pushed a finger through the wire and the wolf licked it until he had to shift gears again.

That had been two years ago, Caleb thought. Two years since he'd come home with Max and Lulu. Two more years with Jessica, when it still looked like there might be a chance. He finished his beer and dropped the empty in the kitchen sink.

The clear cut stretched in all directions across rolling hills. The landscape reminded Caleb of pictures of no-man's land from WWI, a raw wound of pine stumps leaking rosin and tree slash scattered across the ruts left by the skidders and log trucks. Pockets of smoke marked burning slash piles, but the loggers had done little to clean up behind themselves. It would take a lot of work to repair the land and prevent the inevitable erosion, but Caleb knew the Forest Service wouldn't contract out the job. He'd gotten a letter canceling the fire road contract. Their budget had been cut so far that they couldn't even afford fire crews. Three big fires raged in south Mississippi and Alabama alone, over 5,000 acres each, and the combined smoke had cast a yellow-orange tint over the sky. Caleb had stopped in at the Forest Service headquarters to ask about it, but he didn't have any luck. The superintendent, who'd always gotten along well with Caleb when he was working at the newspaper, told him that there were thirty-nine fires in eleven states, over 500,000 acres, and nothing but skeleton crews to fight them.

"Washington is racing to cut every thing down before it can burn," the man said, shaking his head.

A tail of dust plumed from the road just below the other side of the hill. A moment later a pickup crested the hill, going fast, then slammed to a stop, scattering gravel and dusting Caleb's truck. The trucks were facing each other, as if the driver wanted to chat through his window. Caleb pulled his pistol across the seat and nestled it under his thigh.

The driver leaned out of an old two-tone Dodge with a busted grill and a rebel flag plate on the front bumper. Caleb didn't recognize it or the driver. The bed of the truck held a wooden dog box that rocked the truck as the hounds inside jostled around, anxious to be let out. The driver wore a tattered ball cap and a greasy wife-beater tank. His left bicep had the name "Spider" tattooed below a faded pair of flags—American and Confederate—with their staffs crossed. He raised a beer can in salute, and the two other men in the pickup leaned forward to look at Caleb. Caleb nodded.

The driver nodded and glanced off straight ahead, then looked back at Caleb. "Nice day for a drive."

"You bet," Caleb said. He thought now he might have seen the driver hauling pulpwood.

One of the dogs began to howl, setting off the rest.

"Shut up, damn you," the driver yelled at the back of the truck.

The dogs kept going, rocking the whole truck. The man on the passenger side jumped out of the cab and beat on the box with a stick, cursing. He wore sunglasses and a dirty ball cap with the Indian River Paper logo.

"Deer season start early this year?" Caleb asked.

"Naw," the driver said. "We going to run some coyotes, collect the bounty." The man in the middle of the cab slid over to the passenger seat. The back of his shirt was soaked and he looked glad to have the window.

"What's the bounty at now?"

"It's beer money is all."

The man in the passenger seat leaned forward to talk to Caleb. "It's a hell of a fight when they finally corner one. Blood and teeth and fur flying."

"We'll get some money one way or the other," the other guy said. He'd stopped beating the dog cage with his stick and was pointing it at Caleb. "Just got to shoot some stray dogs. Long as they got some fur the co-op don't know the difference."

"You hunting here?" Caleb asked.

"Here's good as anywhere to a dog," the driver said. "You got coyote trouble?"

"I heard you got wolf trouble." This from the man with the stick. All three laughed.

"No trouble to speak of yet," Caleb said

"That so?" the driver said.

Caleb pointed down the hill at the river. "That line of hardwoods down there, that's Black Creek, and everything on the other side is posted. Most of it belongs to either me or my father. Neither of us want dogs on our land."

The driver sipped his beer and tossed the empty on the ground. "Well sir, I ain't never taught them how to read, so I don't know what'll happen if them dogs take a hair to swim. I guess we'll see what happens when it happens."

"I guess so," Caleb said.

"Fuck this, man," the passenger said. "Let's get them dogs out." "You heard the man," the driver said. "He's just looking out for what's his."

"The hell with what's his. This here's national forest and my damn taxes say I own this land, so I'll run my dogs wherever the fuck I want."

"Well I guess I heard that," the driver said. He yelled to the back of the truck. "Sonny Boy, turn them dogs loose, and please ask them to respect this gentleman's property line." He looked at Caleb.

Caleb didn't say anything.

The driver laughed and opened another beer. He stepped out of the truck and stretched.

Caleb cranked the truck and backed out onto the road. One of the men dropped the tailgate and released the latch on the dog pen. A stream of rangy hounds poured out onto the ground, then milled around in a general confusion of biting, growling, pissing, and crapping. The passenger got out on his side and pulled an assault rifle off of the gun rack in the back window. He chambered a round and aimed through the scope at something down the hill and squeezed the trigger, letting off a burst. The shots rang Caleb's ears. The pack of dogs exploded in every direction, sniffing out the scent of something to chase. The man who'd shot turned to look at Caleb and smiled.

Caleb watched the confusion, then shifted and eased down the road. In the rearview mirror he watched the two men turn to watch him drive away. They held rifles with the stocks resting on their hips and the barrels pointed toward the sky.

Jessica meant to call in sick. Her phone was in her purse somewhere, but she had no desire to check messages or her email.

She hadn't finished her sculpture, but it was close enough for her to call done. In a couple of weeks she would show it along with a number of smaller pieces, at which time the Art Department would probably ask her to clean out her office and find something else to do. It didn't matter anymore. She didn't know what she was thinking, trying to pass herself off as an artist. She was a welder, and there was always work for a welder, either here, on the coast, or anywhere she wanted to go.

She thought about all the places she might try. For the first time in a long time she thought of what it would feel like to start over, and the thoughts felt like the relief that comes after a long night of cramping. Alaska was a pipe dream, but she always kept the possibility alive. She often wondered whatever happened to Vann and Annie. Surely Annie had left him by now. She liked the idea of Annie in Alaska, happy, a good husband and kids that would be close to grown now. She liked the idea of Alaska. She had always needed Alaska to be there, even if it felt as far away as the moon. It was like a hundred-dollar bill hidden in her shoulder bag, money for a whim, money for a tank of gas and a motel room should she need the space. It was nothing she ever planned to use, but having it felt like an Ace in the hole should she ever need to play it. Even though the recession was raging and construction was slow, she felt she had enough experience to get on somewhere. Colorado was a possibility, or Phoenix, or even Oregon, Idaho, Montana. The West sounded right to her.

Jessica had started that morning feeling good, fresh on a dream where her mother came to her in the middle of the night and gave her a hug that felt so real, so palpable, that she had sat up fully awake, expecting her mother to be there with her. There was almost an electric charge on the air. Although she didn't normally believe in such things, the dream was so vivid that she had accepted it as real. The dreams had happened before—not with any regularity, but often enough that for the next few nights she looked forward to going to sleep.

At first Jessica's dream had been a nightmare that started in her mother's hospital room the last night of her life. Jessica was with her, but the room was dimly lit and so cold she could see her breath. Nurses worked over her mother, experimenting with her pain, and they sang "Putting on the Ritz." Her mother stared at Jessica over her oxygen mask, wild eyed, but Jessica could do nothing to help.

But after that the dream scene changed and it was Jessica in the bed with her mother sitting in a chair beside her. Her mother had reached over to feel her forehead and brush the back of one hand against her cheek. She stood and said, "I've got to go, but I'll be back in just a little while," and she had leaned over and given Jessica the hug that woke her from the dream.

Her mother always got out the video camera whenever Jessica's brother brought his kids to visit her, and he had given Jessica copies after her mother died.

That morning Jessica had plugged in the first video and watched it all the way through, then went on to the second and the third. She didn't cry like she had in the past, she just watched carefully, hoping for a glimpse of her mother's face, but she was only a voice-over directing the children on the film. Preferring to be behind the camera, her mother had taken hours of those kids at birthday parties, playing in wading pools, opening Christmas presents, but no one ever thought to take the camera away from her and take her picture. The kids were almost grown now, and as their memories began to fade, they would never have any way of remembering what she looked like or how she moved. Thinking about that made Jessica lose her breath, and she lay back on the couch and covered her head with a pillow.

The howling woke Hubert in the night. He got up and dressed and drove the pastures, counting cattle. The moon was new and it wasn't easy to count. He found the newborn calf he'd been waiting on, lying in the tall grass with its mother standing guard over it, but he couldn't rest easy not knowing where the wolves were. He shut off the motor and listened. He convinced himself he could smell the wolves, even on his own property where Caleb had promised they'd never come. They lay their scent all over this valley in their nighttime rambles. After a while he penned the wolves in his mind. It had to do with the absence of noise. Animals freeze up whenever something big, a person or a wolf, comes near in the dark, but stand quiet and the noise will start up again. The sound closes in like the patter of raindrops starting to fall. Tree frogs squawk and whip-poor-wills call. But when the wolves were out of the pen it's like the woods held its breath, and it felt like everything in creation was waiting for the wolves to move on and let them get on about their business.

The business about Caleb and Jessica not living together bothered him. Even though he had never said ten sentences to Jessica on any given day since he had known her, it wasn't right for man and wife not to share the same bed or to live under different roofs. She was a nice enough person, and a damn fine welder —she had kept Hubert's equipment patched and running whenever he needed her. But Caleb had made a mistake taking a woman who didn't want to stay in the house, who didn't act feminine. It was no wonder she ran off since he let her work at the university with those socialist eggheads. It was just a matter of time.

Hubert tried to pray for his son and daughter-in-law, but he felt like he didn't know the right words anymore.

Twenty minutes before sunrise he went out on the porch to listen. It was the first day of deer season for primitive weapons: muzzle loading rifles, bows, and crossbows. *The Walking Dead* had made crossbows popular again, being the weapon of choice against both zombies and people. The national forest—what hadn't been clear cut yet—would be full of hunters in camouflage since the law no longer required hunter orange. The season would make it easy for someone to get on his land and do more damage. Crossbows were deadly silent. Just a matter of waiting beside the pen for Max and Lulu to show themselves, and that would be that. There were shots a long way off at sunrise, but not the ka-thunk of fifty caliber black powder rifles. Fish and Game had stopped checking licenses or deer tags. Every asshole and his brother seemed to be carrying AR-15s with bump stocks or modified to full automatic, and it was safer for the wardens to stay in the office.

Caleb went back to the kitchen and made coffee and leaned against the wall, tired through and through. Hunters would be patrolling in four-wheel drives and ATVs hoping for the easy shot. Others would line the fences overlooking fields and pastures, usually right beside the road. It didn't matter that Caleb's land was posted. Deer and hounds ignored property lines, and the hunters weren't much better. It was safer to stay inside. Anyone could shoot him now and blame it on a hunting accident.

Although most of the hunters only came out for the day, deer camps dotted the national forest, little clusters of camper trailers parked at the end of every fire road. Whatever meat they got was a bonus. Most hunters just wanted to get away from the wife and kids, play Rambo and shoot off whole clips with the touch of a finger, and start drinking early in the day. The deer were relatively safe unless ambushed on opening day, or driven by hounds toward a stand. Scouting game trails and putting out illegal salt licks was hard work. On any given day during the season, Caleb figured eighty percent of the shots he heard were bored hunters taking target practice on tree trunks, squirrel nests, Forest Service signs, or raccoons and possums that happened to wander past.

Hunting season was more dangerous for the people who lived near the forest than it was for the deer. During the regular gun season Caleb wore a hunter orange cap and tried to stay out of the woods. He brought his equipment in from the field and parked it outside the Quonset hut to keep it from getting shot up. Sometimes spent rounds whistled overhead as he worked on his equipment, nearing the end of their two-mile range. Mothers kept their children indoors, but stray bullets sometimes found a way through the wall of a house trailer.

It had been dangerous enough before they legalized automatic weapons. Now hunting season sounded like World War III.

Caleb carried Hubert into town for groceries, and they planned to stop for feed on the way back. He seemed to have bounced back from his most recent round of chemo, though his recovery had taken a couple of days. They didn't talk about the treatments. They didn't talk about the wolves. They didn't talk about Jessica. "Coyotes," Caleb said, slowing the pickup to watch the animals. There were six or seven of them. They kept on about their business, a hundred yards away and trotting with a purpose across a hay field.

"I don't know where they all come from," Hubert said. "We didn't use to have any. I guess they come up from Texas, but I don't know how they cross the river. I guess they could just walk across the railroad bridges if they wanted to bad enough."

"Maybe they were here all along and you just never saw them."

Hubert leaned down and reached under Caleb's seat.

"What are looking for?" Caleb asked.

"Your pistol. Don't you carry it under there?"

"Yeah, but you're not going to use it on those coyotes."

"They ain't wolves."

"It don't matter," Caleb said. He gave the engine gas and pulled away. He watched Hubert's hands as he tried to roll a cigarette. The ends of his fingers were blunt and swollen, a reaction to the chemotherapy. "Don't you think it would be a good idea to stop that?" Caleb asked.

Hubert lit the cigarette. The paper flared but he got a good puff before he tossed the burning paper out the window. They passed through a stretch of woods and then the road opened onto another field. The field was fenced, and spaced every sixty yards along the fence were about a dozen men and boys and a couple of women, waiting for their dogs to run something out into the open. One guy taking a leak against the fence post turned and stared at Hubert and Caleb, not bothering to stop. Caleb slowed and looked the men over, looking for someone he might recognize, but didn't see anyone he knew. The hunters turned and watched them pass, but no one waved. They would be lucky to make it through the day without killing one of the dogs, another hunter, or some poor bastard driving down the road minding his own business.

Caleb slowed the truck and made a wide U-turn, using both ditches to get the truck headed the direction they had come from. The flatbed behind them bounced hard and jerked the pickup, nearly sticking in the ditch, but Caleb gave the truck more gas and pulled it out.

"Damn-it boy," Hubert yelled. "You'll be buying me another trailer."

Caleb ignored him and cruised back that way they had come. He slowed as he neared the field where they had seen the coyotes. At first he couldn't spot them, but then he saw a flash of curled tail in a swath of uncut hay that had been left for the winter, and then he saw the disturbance in the tall grass made by the rest of the pack. Caleb stopped the truck. The coyotes stopped as a pack, unwilling to break the cover of the hay.

"What the hell are you doing? Hubert asked.

Caleb reached under the seat for the pistol and took it out.

Hubert shook his head and looked at the floorboard. He took out his cigarette makings and started another cigarette. "Them coyotes still out there?"

"Yeah."

"I'd like to think you're going to shoot them, help me sleep better at night, but I know better."

"I'll sleep better." Caleb got out of the truck and climbed into the pickup bed. The coyotes were still in the high grass, milling around, and he could see them better now. They were watching him. Caleb steadied his wrist with his free hand and placed the first shot well over the coyotes' heads. The animals danced around in confusion, but still refused to break the cover. Caleb lowered his aim and put the next shot a few feet above the pack. A couple of the animals lay down, trying to hide. Caleb jumped from the bed and crossed the ditch to the fence, stepped between two strands of barbed wire, snagged his coat sleeve, freed himself, and walked into the field toward the coyotes, firing a shot into the ground about every ten steps. The coyotes didn't bolt until he was almost on top of them. Nearly at his feet, they scattered and raced for the tree line. Caleb lowered the hammer on his pistol and walked back to the truck.

Hubert sat with his door open and his feet dangling from the seat. "Feel better?" he asked, as Caleb climbed in and shut his door.

"Yeah, I do," Caleb said. He dropped the clip and reached across Hubert for the box of cartridges in the glove box and reloaded the clip.

"Well, I wish your mother was alive so she could tell me what I done wrong."

Maybe I'm just a bad apple." Caleb put the clip into the pistol and shoved it under the seat. He got the pickup turned around again, taking care to back Hubert's trailer several times so as not to harm it further, then headed back toward the hunters. When he passed them he lay on the truck's horn and waved.

"Give 'em hell, boy," Hubert said. He waved too.

She waited on the edge of the parking lot, standing in the shadow of the trees where she could watch the door to Southern Hall and look out for Caleb at the same time. Now well into September, the weather had yet to cool. She felt conspicuous in her new dress: black, simple, and tight, with spaghetti straps and hemmed well above the knee. The fifteen pounds she'd lost made her body feel thin and powerful and, for the first time in a long time, sexy. She liked the way it felt to move, fluid and graceful. Male students lingered after class and dropped by for office hours more often than they had the year before, which made her feel guilty. Good, but guilty.

The reception for her exhibit wasn't scheduled to begin for another ten minutes, but several of the undergrad art majors had already gone inside, picking up their yellow tickets as they entered the door in order to receive credit for attending the opening, intent on getting to the reception buffet. Faculty and grad students would begin drifting in a little while later, but most of them would arrive late. It was important to give the impression that attending a show was an imposition on their time, and that they had to tear themselves away from their own projects in order to attend. But no one on the faculty wanted to pass up the opportunity for a chance to critique a colleague's work.

Caleb, who was never late for anything, was already fifteen minutes late. She didn't think that he would stand her up—that wasn't his nature. If he didn't plan to come he would have told her. But he wasn't past showing her that he could play separation just as easily as she could. Even though he had appeared willing enough to attend when she'd called him the week before, maybe he'd had time to think about it and had decided that he could show her that he wasn't as desperate as he had seemed in the weeks after she left.

It had been a mistake to invite him, but she had dreaded the thought of walking into the reception alone. Word was out around school that she had moved out, and Jessica knew how gossip ran in the department, but no one had been forward enough to ask her. That she still felt an outsider after so many years stung. She'd never had trouble fitting in on any job—the toughest construction crew only wanted to know that a woman could pull her weight, and her welding had always spoken for her. She dreaded going into the reception and trying to parse criticism out of the compliments and interpretations she was sure to hear. She knew that no matter how hard she tried not to, she would analyze every comment for double meanings and respond to every off-handed compliment with self-deprecating humility. It was a good piece of work, but she would never tell anyone what the sculpture was about.

Just as she was about to give up and go inside, where she would take her place beside the department chair, who would introduce her to patrons and the university administration and heap praises upon her work, Caleb pulled into the parking lot. She set herself, ready for a fight, but as he hurried up the sidewalk her anger cooled. He wore a light blue, button-down shirt and solid tie, sport coat, his best pair of jeans—faded, but without stains—and dark brown leather shoes with Vibram soles. He could pass for an English professor. In his hands he carried a dozen roses wrapped in clear plastic. He offered them to her in explanation.

"Sorry," he said. "I had to go to a couple of grocery stores for your flowers." He leaned forward like he was going to kiss her cheek but drew back.

Jessica took the flowers and leaned into him, breathing in Caleb's smell—hydraulic fluid and wolf, Hubert's cigarettes and stale sweat—as he gave her a light hug.

"I've missed you," she said, "whether you believe it or not."

"Me too." He didn't sound confident, but his eyes widened in surprise and appreciation and he looked at her long enough to look embarrassed when she noticed.

"You look great," he said.

She thanked him and took his hand to walk inside. Caleb's fingers and hands were scarred and calloused, big and powerful. And even though her own hands bore similar scars from her work, Caleb's grip felt good. He had a fine touch—he could write his name in the dirt with the stub of a railroad crosstie clamped in the jaws of a knuckle-boom loader—Jessica had watched him do it one time, delicately manipulating the levers that controlled the hydraulic cylinders of the knuckle boom to scratch out the letters of his name in big block letters.

"Thanks for inviting me," Caleb said.

"Thank you for coming," she said. "You don't know what this means to me."

They got to the door and walked into the gallery.
She felt ready for what lay ahead.

After the reception they drove separately to Stella's for coffee. It was getting close to midnight and the coffee house was thinning out. The baristas had given a last call at 11:30 and were cleaning up. Somebody from Jessica's department had left a few minutes earlier, stopping to congratulate her once more on the success of her opening. She'd waved to a couple of students who'd been at the reception and were making their way out, trying not to make eye contact with their teacher. They had run out of safe things to talk about.

"What exactly are we doing here?" Caleb asked.

She looked at him with a question.

"I've seen you out on a date."

"Bullshit."

"Po-Boy Express, the drive thru. It looked like a date to me."

Jessica looked down at her cup. "That was just talk. Shop talk."

Caleb nodded. "Things just sort of happen. Like a chain reaction, one thing leads to another and when you look back at it, you wonder how you got to here."

"You can stop a chain reaction with one or two good decisions."

They left it at that. Caleb had hoped that the night would end with them back together—the start of the evening had been promising. But as they dropped their guards and let the old familiarity come back, he sensed the conversation deteriorating, and he thought that it was better to end while possibilities still existed.

In the parking lot, where they stopped between the pickup and the Subaru, Caleb said, "I took the slip and ring you left me for a promise that we still have a chance. I'm holding you to that promise. I haven't done everything right, but I've tried to do the right thing every time."

She nodded slowly and said, "I wish I could say the same thing. That I've tried to do the right thing every time." She kissed him on the cheek, and drove off in her Subaru.

She'd promised to drive out to the house in the morning.

The wolves backed away from Jessica. Max lowered his head and stared. Lulu gave out the slightest whimper. Jessica crouched and rested her fingertips on the ground and talked to them in the soothing tones Caleb remembered. Max paced back and forth, stressed. Lulu creeped toward Jessica, her body low to the ground, whining and ready to spring away. She slowly crossed the distance until Jessica could reach out and let her sniff her hand and lightly scratch her head. Max eased closer, testing the air with his nose, until he finally allowed Jessica to touch him. Lulu's tail wagged. Caleb leaned against the gate and watched, pleased.

"Let's take them out," Caleb said. "They've been cooped up the past few days. Do us all good."

Jessica nodded and smiled

Caleb harnessed and leashed Lulu and started on Max. The wolves were eager to go and cooperating for a change. She kneeled beside him to help hold Max in place.

They stopped by Black Creek and tied off the wolves on their chains. The creek looked as unchanged and beautiful as it had ten years ago, when they had been newly married and the world lay before them. Not wanting to look at Jessica, Caleb studied the wolves moving at the ends of their tethers, trying to think of something to say. Max and Lulu moved through the shoal water, snapping at leaves and minnows in the shallow pools, soaking in the water and then rolling on the sandy gravel beach.

"When I was a kid cattle were the first thing I had to think about in the morning and the last thing I saw before dark, and sometimes my dad would have me up with them half the night. Sometimes I think he cared more for those cattle than he did me. I used to figure my life was going to turn out just like his. Maybe all I changed was trading out wolves for cattle."

"Wolves trump cattle."

He thought about the way her leaving had hurt him, and part of him wanted her to feel that same hurt. "Maybe. I don't know that it makes that much difference."

"That wasn't the right answer. That's not what I meant to say."

Caleb scraped the sand with his boot heel. He tossed a handful of pebbles into the water and watched the wolves react. "What I should have said, is I want to come back, but I feel like it should be slow. We've grown apart over the years. A lot of it's my fault."

Caleb didn't want to wait, but he knew it had been a shitty past few years, and neither of them was good about saying what they thought.

"I think we can do things better. I can do things better. But I don't want you to stay unless it's for me. Sooner or later it wouldn't work out anyway." He felt Jessica staring at him, but he didn't want to look.

"Let's say last night was our first date, and today is the second. I've got to go back to town, but can I come back tonight? Maybe bring some supper?"

"I'd like that."

"Yes. Let's go back to the house," Jessica said.

It was late when she came back. Caleb had nearly given up, but he wasn't going to call. Jessica held the flashlight while Caleb buckled on the harnesses. The wolves were difficult, and they circled and bucked and ducked away from Caleb's hands and the straps. He had to straddle Max and hold the wolf between his knees. Max gave a low growl, but he submitted enough to be harnessed, and when Caleb attached the leash he was glad to let the wolf slide out from between his legs. Lulu was easier to harness, so Caleb had Jessica turn off the light so their eyes could adjust to the dark.

Caleb gave the wolves their lead, letting them set the pace and choose the direction. As usual, they first headed up to the ridge above the river, where they stood and tested the air. Max paused every fifty yards to mark his territory. After a few minutes they appeared to be satisfied with what they had smelled and they worked down the ridge to the river, stopping and starting, moving quietly. They strained at the leash more than normal, and soon, they had pushed the boundary of Caleb's land and were onto Hubert's bottomland field covered with the stubble of feed corn for his cows.

At the end of the corn field Caleb pulled back on the wolves. He added extra rope to the ends of the leashes and let them out again, then he sat on a patch of grass. Jessica sat down beside him, close but not close enough. The wolves worked through the stubble, sniffing the ground, their leads knocking down the crop.

Lulu came alert, her eyes focused on a point of ground a few feet in front of her. She took a short quick step, another, and then pounced on something. She came down with stiff front legs held together so that her paws became the head of a club. She dipped her head and came up with a field mouse. Max stood a few feet away, intent on the ground.

They watched the wolves without talking. It had been strained when they started out from the house, but the farther they walked the more it felt like they were falling into their old rhythms, the easy comfort of the first years. They had always been good on those night walks. While one or the other might come home from work tired or angry or nursing a day-long grudge that had festered, walking outside, watching the stars, or listening to the water of Black Creek slide toward the Gulf, had always seemed to put things in perspective and they had never been able to stay angry or hurt for very long. Of course, that was the first years, and they had a lot to talk over now, but they were both satisfied to let the easy rhythm of the wolves take care of this first evening together. After a while Jessica yawned and lay down beside Caleb. He patted his leg and she shifted to lay her head across his thigh. Soon she was asleep.

Caleb watched the wolves and stroked Jessica's hair and let his mind follow a dozen trails. He had envisioned the wolves roaming his property, thinking they would be like big dogs. But they weren't pets in the true sense of the word, and they weren't wild. Caleb felt they were something like him, living in an in-between state where he could never be fully happy, but neither was he sad. Most of the time he was satisfied in the moment, and moments like now were enough.

He thought about God. The idea led to more questions than answers. Most of the religious people Caleb knew seemed to think they deserved answers for everything. But he had been taught that God moved in mysterious ways, which matched his experience. God was a mystery in the Bible. He could be a figure of love in one book, and a raging jealous god in the next. Caleb recalled Hubert's voice, the way he would surprise Caleb in the evenings while Caleb was doing his homework, or sometimes while driving along in the pickup. It was like Hubert had been thinking through a sermon in his mind and suddenly it had boiled over. Hubert's favorite story was from the book of Job, and he often talked about how God allowed the Devil to torment Job, to take away everything except his life. The Devil killed Job's children, made him poor, covered him with sores, and then as Job sat in ashes and scraped at his sores with a piece of broken pottery, his friends came and accused him of some sin he had committed for which he was being punished. Job denied it all. He demanded answers from God. God answered him with questions, asking Job if he understood the complexity of the created world, all the mysteries of science and nature. Job had no answers.

Hubert had the capacity to surprise, and he'd often lecture Caleb: "People want a God of mercy. They don't want the mystery. They bitch at every piece of bad luck and wonder what they had done to deserve God's punishment; they look for a reward on earth rather than the promised one in heaven. People don't know the God of the Bible."

The one thing Caleb could say for Hubert was that he accepted everything the world had done to him without question or complaint. He could complain about the little things—the cost of gasoline or the idiocy of politicians. But the big things, everything from his wife dying to the cancer that was slowly killing him he accepted without fear. No questioning why the God he had placed so much faith in was turning on him. Hubert's faith gave him a peace that Caleb had never known.

Somewhere off in the woods an owl called, and the two wolves raised their heads and listened, then returned to nosing out the scents of the field. A large bird flew over and landed in the trees behind Caleb and Jessica with a soft feather rustling. The wolves were happy. Trucks moved on the highway several miles away and there was a light leaf murmur with the breeze. Jessica's breathing was steady.

After a long time Lulu lay down on a shallow rise. She seemed content to watch the night and catch the smells that drifted across the darkness. Max hunted to the end of the rope and then changed directions and moved away again until the rope caught him short. Jessica moaned and stirred in her sleep and sat up straight. She looked at Caleb as if she didn't recognize him. The puzzlement on her face turned to fear and then slow recognition.

"Bad dream?" Caleb asked.

"How long was I asleep?" Her voice sounded like a child.

"A couple hours. It's okay." Caleb felt like he should reach out and touch her, place a hand on her shoulder to comfort her, but he knew it would be a bad idea.

"I think Lulu might be pregnant," she said.

Caleb paused, wondering what else to say, but then stopped short at the sound of an engine prowling the field on the other side of the tree line. A flash of headlight beams flickered through the trees and briefly touched them, but then the vehicle turned and went back the way it had come.

"My father."

Jessica didn't reply, but he imagined her nodding in the dark.

Caleb stood up and dusted the seat of his pants and waited for Jessica to stand. They gathered the wolves and started back to the pen. Caleb watched Lulu and wondered what Jessica could see that he couldn't.

Jessica stood off to one side, as if she were uncertain what would happen next. Caleb walked over to the bed and turned on the lamp. He motioned for Jessica to turn off the overhead and she flipped the switch.

"This is slow?" he asked.

"Slow enough." She looked at the floor, at the old dresser, at the scratched walls. "It feels like forever. I didn't bring anything to sleep in."

"You left some things here." Caleb pulled back the comforter and took out the blue slip—still neatly pressed from the pressure of the pillow. Her good sign. He held it out and she walked over and took it.

"This will look like a sack on me."

"Maybe you shouldn't wear anything then." Caleb smiled. Jessica gave him an annoyed look, but she blushed.

Caleb pulled a necklace from underneath his shirt. It was made from a leather shoelace and held the ring she'd left him. "I've worn this the whole time."

She held the slip across her front, testing the size. "When you start a new relationship, you're supposed to buy all new lingerie anyway. I guess it's a girl thing."

"It's not a new relationship. It's just a fresh start."

Jessica touched his face with her hand, drawing him toward her, and they kissed. She pulled back and looked at him. "The first night I ever spent here, we talked and talked down by the creek. It was easy to spend the night with you. We just rolled out blankets and fell asleep looking at the stars."

Caleb nodded, remembering.

"We didn't do anything that night," Jessica said. "Just slept. Is it okay if we do that again tonight?"

"Maybe it's best that way," Caleb said.

"Turn out the light."

Caleb turned off the lamp, and they worked their way into the bed and settled there.

It felt like early morning. The coarse cotton sheets felt good against her skin. Caleb was already up and gone, and so she rolled over to his side of the bed and stretched her arms, stretched her legs. She thought about the night and smiled, then turned into the pillow and went back to sleep.

When she awoke again it was mid-morning and she smelled coffee from the kitchen. She went to the window. The day looked crisp, a fall feeling, finally, a day with little humidity and leaves snapping off the trees, a day that felt like the autumn she only saw on television. Jessica played through all the events that had taken place over the past few months, weighing her actions and Caleb's reactions. She thought about the day she left. She thought about everything that had led up to it. It seemed so long ago that it was almost as if she had seen it in a movie. Everything she had done, everything Caleb had done, had been right at the moment. Or at least if not right, it made sense in the moment. Nothing could be taken back, but they still had a chance to do everything right, beginning today. The night before, as she had rolled over to sleep, Caleb had kissed her goodnight and told her that he loved her. She told him the same. Neither of them had used those words in a long time. They had both been cautious to a fault. She thought about how those words made her feel, wrestling with the idea. Sometime in the night she had decided that this was what she wanted: Caleb, the wolves, the university. And waking up with that decision had felt even more right.

Downstairs the rattle of skillet on stovetop and the ring of plates and silverware set on the table was a good sound. She was hungry—hunger like she hadn't felt the past few weeks, where she ate just to fill time, a few bites and then the listlessness of not knowing what she was doing. She felt the hunger of an athlete who'd pushed hard and needed to rebuild muscle. She felt ready to go back to school and tackle the semester. She felt ready to go back to work—another sculpture, her life, Caleb and the wolves. It was the first time she had felt alive in weeks. In the bathroom, she stood in front of the mirror and looked at herself. She looked for what Caleb had seen the night before. She liked the way he had looked at her. And he had felt different. He moved like a man coming out of the desert and finding water. He drank her up. She smoothed her hair, rubbed the sleep out of her eyes, and used Caleb's toothbrush to freshen her mouth. She placed both hands against the wall and stretched her neck and shoulders and arms. She looked over her shoulder at the mirror. Cellulite on her bottom and the cracked ice of varicose veins in her legs. She looked at herself in the mirror and sighed. Middle age. But still, for forty-two, it could be worse.

In the background of the kitchen noise the radio was tuned into a swap show for equipment, dogs and goats, chores. It was the sound of home, of her mother cooking breakfast on a lazy Sunday morning with her father sitting at the table sipping coffee and reading the paper, the sound of pancakes and sausage and eggs with a big glass of orange juice to cut the hangover from sleeping in too late. She slipped into one of

Caleb's flannel shirts and buttoned it walking down-stairs.

"Sorry I've been so lazy this morning," Jessica said, as she stepped into the kitchen, but she stopped short.

Caleb stood at the stove turning sausage patties with a spatula, and Hubert sat at the kitchen table rolling a cigarette.

Hubert's eyes, the only thing vibrant in his skeletal frame, bored into her. He looked on the verge of a question. Caleb cut his eyes at Hubert, a what-are-the-odds look, smiled and put down the spatula.

"I was about to come up and get you," he said. "Or warn you." Jessica turned. "I've got to get dressed," she mumbled.

"Don't run away," Hubert said. "We've already waited the morning for you."

Jessica paused and looked at him, clutching the shirt at her neck. He'd grunted over the phone on the rare occasions he'd called. Gave her a curt nod whenever their vehicles met on the road, but that was it. She felt like a teenage girl caught necking in the back seat of a car, staring into the beam of a flashlight pinning her to the seat.

"You still welding?"

Jessica blinked, surprised. "Yes."

"My son busted up my trailer some. Thinks he's the *Dukes of Hazzard*. Reckon you could do some patching on it?"

"Yeah, I can do that." She looked at Caleb.

Hubert looked satisfied. "I finally got the boy to start breakfast and it looks like it's done. Pour yourself some coffee and have a seat." He pushed out a chair for her with his foot.

Jessica looked at Caleb.

"I'll get your coffee," he said. Jessica sat down beside Hubert.

Hubert shook his head and looked at the cigarette in his hands. His eyes were a watery blue. He looked up at Caleb. "You going to cook them eggs sometime today? I've got cattle to tend to."

The old man waited until Caleb poured Jessica's coffee, then held out his own cup. He gave Jessica what passed for a smile. She wondered what it was like to watch the world slip out of your hands and know that there was nothing in your power to stop it. It probably wasn't much different for Hubert than for anyone else, though. Nothing ever worked out the way it was planned. No one ever acted the way you expected. It must be obvious to someone Hubert's age. He had had a lifetime to grow cynical. He had seen enough of the world to understand that he had no lasting effect on anything. It would hurt to think about the world going on long after you were gone. Jessica almost felt sorry for the old man. Almost.

Jessica could see Caleb in Hubert's face, and she wondered what it would be like to watch Caleb's face grow into his father's. She wondered what her own face would become, since she had never seen her own mother as a truly old person. If they stayed together, would she and Caleb bicker and growl at one another, moan about their aches and pains, sit in matching armchairs in the evening? Would this be the life they lived—a small house in the woods with wolves at the door and the smell of diesel fuel and hydraulic fluid on the air? Would one of them have to bury the other way too soon and be left to live a life as lonely as Hubert's? As lonely as her own life these past months? There were so many questions, and the answers weren't always pretty. But then Caleb touched her on the shoulder as he sat down to breakfast beside her. A light touch, a smile, a tender man. Jessica smiled back and sipped her coffee, feeling the warmth all the way to her stomach.

As September ground on there were signs that summer was breaking and cooler fall weather was in sight. The highs still fell in the 90s, but the morning air felt cleaner, and skies a high pressure blue, replacing the warm damp heat that blanketed the summer. A hint of leaves changing color, whether from fall or the continuing drought. Hubert was in a holding pattern, having finished his first round of chemotherapy. Other than the days Caleb took his father in for treatments, they saw the old man only when they passed his pickup on the road, or parked in his field with his cattle. Jessica stayed in town a couple of times a week on nights before early classes.

Caleb sensed she had been in a better mood since the reception. While she had been worried about what the other faculty might say about the piece, their comments were positive and she believed, sincere. She told Caleb that the sculpture had wrung her out physically and emotionally. It was the best work of her life, and she just didn't think that she could ever do any better. Caleb had watched the sculpture grow from a year earlier, when she started with an eight by twenty panel of sheet metal to which she applied heat and a cable spool to roll into a long curve. She had cut shapes out of copper, brass, bronze, aluminum, and steel and welded and soldered them onto the panel. As it took shape, Caleb had a vague notion of what she was trying to do. She set up a scaffold in front of the piece and he watched her move across it, dabbing chemicals, smoothing edges with a torch or file, smacking a reluctant piece of metal with a hammer. She used a torch to flame paint the copper, altering the heat and duration to consume oxygen on the surface of the metal, drawing out deep reds, blues, and purples, painting on solutions of salt and vinegar to add greens and turquoise. She worked with ferric nitrate, ammonium, and sulfurated potash to bring out more color. She had explained the chemistry behind the colors, but Caleb had always been content to just watch her absorption in the problem of the moment.

After she moved the sculpture to town, she had added a bridge crossing the Mississippi, steel rods wired with tiny LED lights that wouldn't overwhelm the sunset colors. The river itself was a flat copper and bronze sheet heat-treated to bring out the reflection of the setting sun on the water. Natchez was bathed in the warm light, and it glowed with tiny lights and the shadows of the contour of the bluff. Seeing Jessica's vision for the sculpture fulfilled moved Caleb in a way he had never expected. He had felt something like it at different times in his life: a few sunrises and sunsets had come close, though he couldn't explain the reasons; seeing his byline for the first time in the newspaper; a few times at church when he had been moved by something that might have been the spirit; walking with the wolves and Jessica under a full moon when everything flowed together in perfect unison. He had read about what American Indians called "medicine," those moments when a warrior felt completely in tune with the world around him, both physically and mentally and spiritually. He thought Jessica had it.

He hoped he was getting his own medicine.

All the way to the hospital Hubert leaned against the passenger door and struggled to breathe. He wouldn't even move his head when Caleb asked him a question. When Hubert hadn't answered his phone, Caleb had gone looking for him. He'd found him around 9 p.m., slumped in his pickup in a pasture, his cattle grazing around him, expecting to be fed. The ambulance bay was full, so Caleb parked in a doctor's space and went around to get his father. Hubert responded enough to stand, but he couldn't walk. Caleb lifted him and carried him toward the door. He was surprisingly heavy for a man so shriveled up.

Inside, a woman in scrubs helped Hubert into a wheelchair while Caleb explained his father's condition. Hubert slumped and closed his eyes, his breathing ragged. They sat in the ER waiting room for ten minutes—Caleb noted the stares of the injured and sick and their families as they tracked each new patient and calculated who was next in line. Children played on the floor, sucking on plastic bottles of Coke and eating potato chips. Bored relatives scrolled through their phones or eyed the television playing a *Little House on the Prairie* rerun. A girl in flowery scrubs came out and wheeled Hubert into the back. Caleb followed, trying not to make eye contact with anyone as he headed toward the automatic doors.

A couple of techs lifted Hubert onto a gurney and wheeled him into a curtained exam area. Caleb sat in a plastic chair in the corner and watched the staff work.

The voices of other patients and their family came from the adjacent curtained exam areas. Nurses and techs came and went, taking temperature and blood pressure, removing Hubert's clothes and replacing them with a gown. Someone came in and asked questions about insurance. Caleb found an insurance card in Hubert's wallet, but he had to swipe his own credit card for the copay. After a few minutes a doctor came back with Hubert's charts and strapped an oxygen line under his nostrils. Hubert began to breathe easier and eventually drifted to sleep. The doctor explained that they wanted to do some blood work and see where the white cell counts were, and other factors that Caleb didn't really follow. Hubert hadn't talked about his condition. Cancer was explanation enough.

Caleb moved the pickup to a parking lot. Cumulus clouds were building in the west, weather coming in from Texas and Louisiana. It was warm and he hoped rain would cool things off, wash the dust off the brush that lined his gravel road, raise the level of Black Creek a few inches and wash the shoals. In the few clear spots of the sky he picked out stars. Orion's belt. That, along with the Big and Little Dipper was about all he remembered from childhood stargazing, when things like constellations seemed to matter. The town was quiet except for a little highway traffic noise, and Caleb thought about how nice it felt to be awake in a sleeping city. A black man wearing a New Orleans Saints t-shirt leaned against a concrete column a few feet away, smoking. Caleb bummed a cigarette. The man cut his eyes at him, but he took his pack and fished out a cigarette. Caleb thanked him and asked for a light.

He took in a breath and felt the smoke hit him like a drug. He'd never liked menthols. His fingertips and lips tingled and his head felt light.

"Who you here for?" Caleb asked.

"My wife's having a baby," the guy said.

"A baby. That's exciting."

"Ain't nothing but a step," the guy said, shrugging his shoulders.

"What are the Saints going to do this year?"

"Saints? Shit." The last word drawn out to three syllables.

He flicked his cigarette away and walked inside.

Caleb finished the cigarette and enjoyed the night air, reluctant to go back into the hospital. Jessica didn't answer, so he texted "In room, waiting for blood work."

When he went back his father sat up in bed and the doctor told him that Hubert was responding well to the oxygen. He turned to Hubert and said, "We want to keep you at least the night, Mr. Vogel. I want to consult with your oncologist. He might keep you a couple days until you build up some strength."

"A man never got stronger laying in bed," Hubert said. "I got things to see about."

"Your son will have to take care of your house," the doctor said. "We've got to take care of you."

Hubert complained some more, until he ran out of breath and had to stop talking. The doctor made some notes on the chart and left. Caleb sat down beside Hubert and slouched in his chair.

Hubert appeared to doze off. Caleb stared at the curtain separating them from the rest of the ER. Voices of other patients and their family, whispering, laughing, crying. Someone in the next curtain started to snore. He was startled when Hubert spoke to him.

"I never told you much about my step-daddy, did I?" Hubert asked.

Caleb looked at his watch. Midnight. He wondered what Jessica was doing.

"No."

Hubert spoke deliberately, with his eyes closed tight and his sentences drawn out between long pauses to breathe. "He used to come home drunk and tear up the house, beat up mamma. He was mad about everything. He tried to get to me but she used to wake me up when she heard him coming down the road and we'd go hide. I was too little to do anything about it, but Mamma had a brother who knew what was going on. That man, her own brother, never did anything to help us. Figured that back then a woman belonged to her man. She told me that God would look down on us and help us out, but he never did anything for us either. I should have done something, but I was no use to her."

He dozed off. Caleb listened to the hospital sounds. "You know I'm dying, don't you?"

Caleb nodded, even though Hubert's eyes were still closed. "Don't let me die in here, you hear me? I want to be outside."

"It's not down to that yet. You'll be home in a day or two. I'll check your cattle."

"What I said before. I was too little to do anything, and my uncle was too sorry to do anything. My step-daddy took any chance of joy out of my mamma's life, and there wasn't much there to begin with. If I'd a been a man, or at least bigger than a runt, my mother wouldn't never have had to climb out a window in the middle of the night to keep a drunk from kicking the shit out of her or me. Some people just want to take what you got and they keep on taking 'til they got it all."

Hubert folded up like a closed book, his sermon delivered, and Caleb saw that he was done for the night. He patted his father's leg and said good night, but Hubert didn't open his eyes. Caleb found his father's shirt, which someone had stuffed into a plastic bag with his other clothes. He took out the tobacco and cigarette papers, then eased through the curtains.

Caleb unscrewed the top off the bottle of bourbon and poured some into a glass and pulled out a kitchen chair. His body had felt weightless as he lay in bed— "too tired to sleep," Jessica had always called it, quoting her father. The bourbon warmed him and gave him something like energy. The house creaked. He rolled a cigarette from Hubert's makings and lit it. He thought about how easy it was to start smoking again and thought he ought to do something about it.

He had spent a good part of the day sitting with Hubert in a hospital room, watching him sleep, though occasionally he'd wake up, confused for a moment, and ask about his cows. "Keep them wolves penned," he said.

The doctor had come in toward the end of the day. Hubert was asleep, so he told Caleb, "I'm not going to promise you that your father will improve. He's had a lot of damage to his lungs over the years, and I don't think he slowed down and acted like he was sick during the chemotherapy treatments. All of that takes a toll on the body. He's a tough man to keep going like he has. He must feel like hell every day."

Caleb tried to think of the important questions he should ask, but nothing came to him. "This is it then?" he asked.

"I don't think so," the doctor said, looking at his clipboard. "He may get a little stronger with rest. He may even get to go home tomorrow. He can breathe oxygen there as well as he can here. I wouldn't expect him to resume an active lifestyle, and I don't think I would recommend any more treatments. I don't think he's strong enough for that."

"Just waiting to die?"

"He has time to get his business wrapped up."

Caleb thanked the doctor and then went back in the room and sat next to his father, who was dozing behind his oxygen mask. The television on the wall was playing the Weather Channel. A big tropical storm out in the Atlantic, aiming for the tip of Florida. Hubert's mask fogged and cleared, fogged and cleared.

Their time on the Tennessee river--having never been farther than Jackson or Biloxi, since Hubert didn't like to get off his home patch, seeing the foot-hills of the Appalachians--had been Caleb's Alaska. They had fished the Neshoba, the river that Black Creek flowed into, lots of times. Hubert kept a jon-boat and a little Evinrude, and to Caleb it was a big river, widening to a hundred yards in the big bends, and deep in places. Hubert liked to set out trotlines across the width of the river and run them until he'd filled his cooler with catfish. When he was satisfied, he'd pull up his trotlines and they'd go back to the boat launch and clean the fish. Hubert had driven a nail into a tree, where he'd hang the fish's head on the nail, make a couple of skin slits below the head, and pull the slick skin off with pliers. Caleb's job had been to gut the skinned fish, cutting a vertical slit in the belly and scooping everything inside out with his fingers, then throw the skinned and gutted fish into the clean cooler and ice them down. But the Ten-nessee was big water. Dammed every fifty or hundred miles, the river had expanded over its valley, so that in places it was a mile wide. They fished in the corner where three states came together, and Caleb liked looking at the distant green line wrapped in the hazy light of summer and thinking, "That's Tennessee, and that's Alabama." The names themselves, especially Tennessee, sounded exotic, calling up images of hillbillies and moonshine, or the mythology of Alabama football and Bear Bryant. Hubert liked to stay out all night and all day. "If I'm driving all the way to Tennessee, I'm filling up my freezer when I get home," he said. Red and green running lights of other boats bobbed on the river, sometimes a couple of miles off, rising and falling with the movement of the big water, blinking like lights on a Christmas tree. Riverboats pushing strings of barges rolled up and down the current, the big searchlight sweeping the water and the banks, and the big diesel engines throbbing over the wash of the wake. Hubert would stay on his lines until the last possible minute, before dropping the line and cranking the Evinrude and puttering out of the path of the oncoming barges, muttering about how they would drive away all the fish and the expense of having to bait up after the barge. After the barges and riverboat passed, the waves thrashed the fourteen-foot boat. Caleb would hold to both gunwales and watch the lights of the towboat recede, relaxing when the quiet returned. Hubert smoked his cigarettes in the back of the boat until the water was calm enough to crank up and go back to the float that marked the beginning of the trotline. They came away from the trip with enough fish to fill the deep freeze on the back porch and invite the whole church to a fish fry with what couldn't fit in the freezer. Nothing made Hubert happier than a full freezer.

Hubert moved in his sleep and groaned, opened his eyes for a moment and blinked. His eyes looked weak and unfocused without his glasses, beady, suspicious, and sleepy. He dropped back into sleep for a few minutes but another groan and he was awake. He blinked for a while, then patted the bedside table for his glasses. His eyes snapped into focus when he put them on and he took the mask off his face.

"What did the doctor say? He been here?"

Without his hat, Hubert looked like an owl. "He said you might get to go home tomorrow, on oxygen."

"What else did he say?"

Caleb repeated what the doctor had said. Hubert stared at the television on the wall above Caleb's head. He nodded and turned toward the wall. Caleb sat in the chair and leaned back, fatigue washing over him like the first flush of heat exhaustion, a dry chill and nausea. He remembered he hadn't slept since the start of the day before. He closed his eyes and was nearly asleep when Hubert's voice brought him back.

"Wake up, Boy." He'd rolled back over to face Caleb. "Look in your mother's old jewelry box and you'll find a safe deposit key. Go to the bank and get my papers—they got your name—then you find my lawyer and tell him to get over here and earn his money. I got to straighten out my will. I give everything to that slick-talking preacher on the television."

"Quitman?"

"I was mad about those wolves."

Hubert replaced his mask and held it in place for a few moments. Caleb turned to leave, but Hubert motioned with his hand for him to stay. He stared at Caleb over the mask. Caleb was afraid of what he might say next. He wasn't ready for emotion, or what passed for emotion with Hubert.

Hubert pulled off the mask and cleared his throat. "Did you feed my cattle today?"

"Yeah."

He put the mask back on and adjusted the strap behind his head. He lay back on the pillow and waited for Caleb to leave.

Early afternoon, and the sky glowed yellow like aged varnish. The hurricane was a hundred and eighty miles from the mouth of the Mississippi after skipping across the Florida peninsula north of Miami. It had grown into a Category Five, and predictions for land-fall ranged from the Florida Panhandle to Texas. It was looking more and more like Louisiana, and Caleb knew from experience that the rotation of the storm would push the storm surge to the east of wherever the eye landed. Tropical-force storm winds extended two-hundred-and-thirty miles from the eye, so Biloxi and Bay St. Louis were already getting hit. The seas in the Gulf were running at sixteen feet ahead of the hurri-cane, and they had already evacuated most of the off-shore oil rigs and put out small craft advisories. Inside the Mississippi sound, which was protected by barrier islands out in the Gulf, the gambling barges in Biloxi and Gulfport had been pulled free of their moorings and floated into better protected waters.

The order to evacuate the coast had come at 8 a.m. Living forty-five miles in from the coast, Caleb was worried. The storm would bring high winds and tornados and the creek would flood. Jessica was still in town. She'd put off coming home until the last minute, citing her parents riding out Lucinda in Biloxi and how she rode out Julia in the French Quarter, the brand of coastal optimism that always irritated Caleb. There was more traffic on the cellular network than the band-width could handle, and their calls kept dropping. It didn't matter how much food, gas, water, batteries, and generators he had if he didn't know she was safe.

The streets in town were choked. The motels along Highway 49 filled up all the way to Jackson, forcing coastal evacuees further north. Wal-Mart had been run, cleaned out of batteries, water, canned goods, portable radios, and ammunition. Getting Hubert home from the hospital was a test of patience worthy of Job. Three of the four lanes of the highway were dedicated to northbound traffic, with the one open lane reserved for emergency vehicles. Highway patrol and sheriff's cruisers ran up and down the shoulders, blue lights blazing, forcing line skippers to get back into the traffic lanes and keep the shoulders open. National Guard soldiers, looking self-important in their uniforms and traffic cop duties, sat in their Humvees, dipping Copenhagen or smoking cigarettes. In a few hours all Southbound traffic would be closed off. The mayor of New Orleans had ordered an evacuation, and all the cities along the Mississippi coast were emptying.

Caleb crept along the single southbound lane, listening to Hubert complain about the hospital and fume at the traffic and worry about his cattle. He complained about the bottle-asses plugging up the road and the camel jockey doctors who'd held him captive at the hospital. Hubert hated the government; he hated the coasters who'd filled their cars floorboard to ceiling with children, pets, and household crap; he hated everything. Caleb thought about the ones left behind, those too poor or too sick to get out. They would suffer. He thought about the hurricane parties gearing up on the coast and in the French Quarter, the die-hards who were too lazy, or too suspicious of the government to obey the evacuation. Like Jessica and her parents;

they'd waited out plenty of hurricanes, claiming they were never as bad as predicted, or else they just missed. Why pack up their lives and leave the rest to weather and looters. The coast was full of survivors from the big storms, a lot of them old codgers who'd drank and danced through the storm and the storm surge with hardly a scratch or a drop of rain, claiming bravery for stupidity.

Caleb kept the radio tuned to the weather and listened to the predictions crackling with static. Thirty-foot waves in the Gulf with rogue waves measured at fifty feet, one-hundred and twenty-five mile mile-per-hour winds, low pressure and warm Gulf water sucking more energy into the storm. Every mile or so a highway patrol or National Guard stopped them, wanting to know where they were headed. Caleb had to show a driver's license to prove they were heading home and not looting. When he tried to turn off the highway heading east, it took an hour to cross the three lanes of traffic as he forced his bumper into the narrow gaps between cars. He had to turn wide right and cut back to the north to force a merge, scraping bumpers and scratching paint. The pickup towered above a Corolla as Caleb forced his way into a second lane of traffic. The man driving got out of his car screaming and cussing, ready to fight. Hubert rolled down his window and pointed Caleb's pistol in his face. The man retreated to his car and continued to blow his horn and scream profanity while his children cowered in the back seat.

"Nothing left to lose?" Caleb asked.

"Man shouldn't act like that in front of his children. It ain't Christian. I ought to pull him out of there and make him pray."

Caleb shook his head and laughed.

"What?" Hubert looked offended.

"The irony."

Hubert waved him off and wondered aloud about his cattle. "I got one ready to drop a calf," he said. "I hate to see that in a storm."

"It's all part of God's nature."

"Don't make fun of what a man believes," Hubert said. He tipped his hat toward the man in his car.

Caleb leaned over and looked past Hubert. The man gripped the steering wheel with both hands, though the vehicles hadn't moved more than a few inches in fifteen minutes. Caleb tried Jessica again, but the call went straight to voicemail.

"You don't believe in a world with a Creator, that's your business. You're old enough to make your own decisions now."

Caleb nodded and eased the truck forward a few inches.

When they got close to the house Hubert demanded to be taken home. Caleb argued with him, told him he was too weak to be by himself in a hurricane, but Hubert wouldn't let it rest. He helped the old man settle himself and checked on the cattle, laying out hay and feed. Caleb knew they would lay down in the pastures and suffer, but they would probably be okay. Hauling hay reminded him too much of growing up, but there was something comforting in the work, tossing hay bales out of the bed and busting them open for the cattle pushing in.

By the time he got home Jessica's Subaru was parked in front of the house. He went inside and found her, making a point to not show how worried he had been. Then they went down to the pen. Max and Lulu were anxious with the weather. Lulu dug deeper into her den. Max prowled inside the chain link, whimpering.

Caleb and Jessica tried to hold hands as they walked toward the river, but Max and Lulu jerked them through their leads and they gave up. Jessica sang an old Jimmy Buffett song: "Trying to Reason with Hurricane Season."

They went into the creek to wash off after making love on the sand bar. The surreal pre-storm light, the trickle of water on the shoal, and branches popping and cracking made it reckless and good, despite the grit. Max and Lulu waded in the shallows snapping at floating twigs and leaves. Jessica nestled inside Caleb's legs, her back supported by his chest and her head resting on his shoulder; he leaned against the current, his arms straight behind him and hands against the gravel of the shoal. Her breasts floated just below the surface, pale. Lightning bugs flickered green and yellow against the darkening woods. Fast-moving clouds skidded across the sky against an early rising moon. The wind whistled through the canopy of the trees sixty feet above, swirling the tree limbs and stripping off the leaves so they fell in a quiet shower, but the air above the creek was still. The water fell toward the Gulf of Mexico, the current slowed slightly by Caleb's shoulders. Sand and pebbles shifted beneath him.

"I could sit like this all night," Jessica said.

"Me too." Caleb tossed a few rocks to discourage snakes, though Max and Lulu, chained and wading downstream, usually drove anything dangerous away. He thought for a few minutes about how to best phrase his question, but he couldn't put into words what he really wanted to ask. Moving her hair from one of her shoulders, he said, "So, where are we, exactly? A lot's happened this summer."

Jessica stiffened. She was quiet for a long time.

"We're in Black Creek, naked, talking, relatively happy?"

"I've been waiting for the other shoe to drop."

"These are the kind of conversations that make me want a cigarette. A coffee and cigarettes kind of talk."

Caleb laughed. He wrapped one arm around her waist. "I'm glad we quit."

"What about everything else?"

"I'm not unhappy." She placed one hand over his hand. "Can we not make it more complicated than that right now?"

Caleb squeezed her waist. "The hurricane feels closer than what they said on the weather."

Jessica scooted a little deeper. Her shoulders were under water and leaning against him. Caleb brushed a strand of her wet hair away from his nose and leaned forward and cupped her left breast in his other hand. She let it rest there for a moment before moving his hand to her waist.

"Dexter," she said. "That's too nice for a hurricane."

"A lot of mild names for so many bad storms. I can't believe they went all the way through to Zoe and had to start over."

"I remember the big ones growing up." Jessica counted them off on her fingers: "Pearl, Sandy, Harley, Pandora, Bonnie, Scout. They ought to name them all Killer."

"Do you remember Lucinda?"

"A little. I guess I was six or seven. I slept through most of it, but my mom said she and my dad sat up all night playing rummy by candlelight. Where were you?"

"Right here. Hubert doesn't run from hurricanes either. Another family from our church came over and we all got in the hallway. They lived in a little aluminum trailer about the size of my kitchen. They had a girl I liked—she was three or four years older than me, and I thought she was beautiful—and I wanted to sit next to her. It was my chance to look cool, like the teenagers, but my mother made me sit next to her instead. She kept saying, 'You sit next to me so I can pull you out of here if the walls collapse.' I kept wondering how she was going to pull me out if the walls fell in. She was already dying and we didn't know it."

"You wanted to look good for your little girlfriend," Jessica said. "You were nine?"

"Something like that. The winds were just like this. Random, hard. Blowing from one direction, then the other. That house rattled like washboard road. We sang hymns and my father read from the Bible, all that spooky apocalyptic stuff from the Old Testament that he likes so much. When it was my turn I got smart and read about the destruction of Jerusalem, that part about the walls of the city being torn down and people having to flee to the hills to escape. Judgement Day. Ole Hubert snatched the Bible out of my hands and I was sure I'd get a whipping later. A big wind came through and knocked some trees down on the house. I could feel them hitting. Like bombs going off. The house was groaning and it busted out some windows."

"What did it sound like?" Jessica asked.

"Like a forest fire. When the fire heats up the air around a pine tree it vaporizes all the flammable chemicals in the needles, and all of a sudden the tree simultaneously combusts. The whole canopy will go up in a few seconds. A whooshing sound, like a jet taking off. Then the fire will spread from treetop to treetop and it just becomes a continual roar."

"It's like that 'You Might Be a Redneck If' joke: 'If you've ever been on the ten o'clock news and you say the tornado sounded like a freight train.'"

"Nobody ever bothered to ask me what it sounded like," Caleb said. The cloud shadow darkened, making Max and Lulu nearly invisible in the shallow water a few feet away. Both animals focused on some noise or scent they'd picked up from down the river. Caleb listened. Wind, trees creaking, leaves fluttering, water flowing, knock of tree branch on branch. The wind smelled like rain.

"So, what happened after the trees hit the house?" Jessica asked.

"It got real quiet. The wind and the rain stopped. You could've heard the birds outside if there had been any. My dad stood up and looked at the ceiling and the walls, listening real hard. All we had was a Coleman lantern and his shadow took up the whole hallway.

"My mother started praying out loud. She kept saying 'Deliver us from your wrath oh God,' but my father shushed her. He said, 'It's the eye of the hurricane. We're in the middle of the eye, but all hell's fixing to break loose when the back side passes over.' That other woman started to scream. She was holding her baby and trying to get up and get out the door. I guess she couldn't take it anymore. Her husband stood up and punched her and she kind of cradled that baby in her arms and fell back against the wall and slumped to the floor. I thought she was dead."

Jessica muttered something.

"That girl I liked—her name was Tina—she just started giggling when she saw her mother. I guess she went a little crazy too. Her daddy reached down and picked up the baby and set it in Tina's arms. She rocked it like a baby kitten."

"She had a wonderful father."

"They cut pulpwood. That's just the way they were. That man'd have his whole family out there picking up sticks and stacking them on the pulpwood truck as soon as they were old enough to walk. She was tough."

"She had to be."

"Yeah. Her daddy looked at my mother and me, sort of embarrassed, and said, 'Maybe we ought to pray some more, Hubert,' and my dad said okay. So that man stood over his wife and prayed for deliverance."

Jessica tensed under his arms.

"That's when it got bad, I guess. Made the front of the hurricane look like a light wind. I'd just seen *The Wizard of Oz* and I swore the house was being lifted off the ground. Trees were falling all over us and the roof started to leak. We probably had a couple of inches of water on the floor. The mother woke up and started screaming again, but her husband just kept on praying. My dad stood there bracing the walls with both arms, like he thought he could keep the house standing."

"Were you scared?"

"I guess I was, but I don't really remember. I didn't think much about dying. My dad said dying didn't matter if you lived right."

"The philosopher of the ages," Jessica said.

"He believes it."

Jessica grunted, then flinched as a treetop snapped in the woods and crashed to the ground. "So whatever happened to that family?"

"There wasn't anything left of their place. There were knocked down trees all over. Like a box of spilled matches. The woman and the baby went to stay with her sister or somebody. The man kept Tina and her little brother to help him cut the trees off the trailer, but one of them fell on him and pinned him to the ground. Tina sent the brother after my dad, and she stayed there and tried to cut the tree off him with a chainsaw. I think that's what she was trying to do. When me and my dad got there he was near cut in half and she was standing over him laughing."

"Jesus," Jessica said. She shook her head.

"That's what my dad kept saying, 'Jesus. God help us.' Tina and the rest of them went to live over in Alabama. I never saw her after the funeral."

Jessica raised and turned to look back at Caleb, then lay back against him.

The wind dropped below the treetops and sent a cool breeze rippling across the water. A few rain drops fell around them, and then grew into a drizzle. The rain felt cold against the warm creek. The rain-drops were fat and noisy. Max and Lulu still focused on something upriver, staring quietly, and then both wolves began to growl.

"What's wrong?" Jessica asked.

Caleb backed away from Jessica and stood up, straining to hear over the splashing rain. Finally, he was able to pick up the sound of hounds working their way down the trail from the wolf pen. "Get your clothes on," he said, starting for his clothes and gun.

Jessica scrambled to her feet and went to the bank. She dressed quickly as barking filled the woods, echoing in the hollows and bouncing off the water. It sounded like twenty, but surely there couldn't be that many. She heard Caleb chambering a round into the pistol. Despite the rain and the amber light of the setting sun, the moon was out and it glowed weirdly though the racing cloud cover. The light was sharp and every detail was clear, and she thought briefly about how she could capture it in metal. Caleb was looking at her, his expression determined. Definitely not scared. He lowered the hammer and tucked the gun in the waist of his pants.

Caleb put the wolves back on lead and dropped the log chains. He handed her Lulu. The wolf strained at the leash, dragging her through the shallows to meet the approaching hounds. Jessica fell to her knees in waist deep water and the wolf skidded her until she finally got her feet and managed to stand. She set her feet and jerked back on the leash, turning Lulu a somersault. The wolf ignored her, rolled to her feet, and tried to move downstream again, but this time Jessica was able to wrap the leash a turn around a cypress stump and hold her. Lulu's ears stood straight and her fur between her shoulder blades raised like a stiff spine. Caleb caught up and secured Max's leash to the stump. Max pulled against his leash, rocking the stump. Lulu whined, low and scary.

"What should we do?" Jessica asked.

The way Caleb looked at her made her realize it was a stupid question. The dogs were another force of nature, just like the hurricane out in the Gulf.

Splashing downstream. Jessica noticed the wind like it was a new thing, and realized it carried the sound of the dogs with it. Stinging raindrops pricked her face. The clouds raced across the face of the moon, lighting the river bottom like a strobe light. Further downstream men were shouting, whooping at their dogs and cursing the woods as they tried to keep up. Max and Lulu twirled at the ends of their leashes, entangling themselves, rocking the stump loose from the sand that embedded its roots.

Job. It was an appropriate book for the weather because, after all, Job's troubles had started with tornadoes striking the house where his sons and daughters were feasting, killing them all. Hubert listened to the wind shake his house and thought about the book of *Psalms*, where King David had written:

"He makes winds his

messengers,

flames of fire his
servants."

He wondered what the wind had to tell him tonight. Probably nothing. Maybe, that it was time to go out in the storm and let God have his way. The will was finished—signed and notarized, giving everything to Caleb, cattle records filed, savings account and insurance policies locked in the safe-deposit box. His lawyer knew where everything was, and Caleb wouldn't have any trouble sorting out his affairs. He'd already made the arrangements at the funeral home—everything paid for.

There were worse ways to die than in a storm. God spoke to Job out of the whirlwind. Jesus calmed the waters. He would be with his cattle, and that's where anybody who knew him would expect to find him. Out in the field with his cattle. He rolled another cigarette and thought about it, had just about made up his mind when the shooting started down at the river. It was just far enough away, dimmed by the wind and the rain, that he thought it was firecrackers.

Hubert lit his cigarette and stood up and waited for the dizziness to pass. When he could walk, he pulled on his boots and headed out the door, pausing only long enough to pull on his raincoat and pick up the shotgun from the corner by the door.

The barking stopped but the dogs crashed through the woods, hunting now on sight rather than scent, killers, now, rather than hunters. A dog burst over the bank like something out of a movie, launching itself twenty feet into the water. There were four or five behind it, maybe more. Long and skinny, starved looking, the lead dog reached the sandbar and streaked toward them, mouth open and tongue hanging to one side, teeth barred. Caleb tracked and shot it in the chest and it tumbled over and over and lay fifteen feet away in shallow water.

The other dogs slowed with the gunshot but kept coming. Caleb pulled out his pocket knife and cut Lulu's lead. The wolf tumbled over with the unexpected freedom and lay flat on the sandbar. He cut Max's lead. The wolf trotted around the edge of the sandbar, circling behind the first two dogs, who had stopped a few feet from Lulu, posturing in an unpredictable dog standoff. Their growls were mechanical. Thousands of canine signals being transferred: scents, sounds, body language ranging from the posture of the body to the raised hackles on their backs.

One of the dogs broke from its crouch and ran over Lulu. Lulu got to her feet and lifted the dog by the throat. A second dog moved in on Lulu's flank and bowled her and the dog over in a tangling snarling mess. Max came up from behind and the fight congealed into a confusion of shadow and movement in the quickening darkness, buzzing, white eyes, clicking teeth.

Two or three more dogs rushed into the scrum. Caleb tracked them with the gun but they moved too fast to shoot. Another dog circled the pack and he fired quickly. It limped away, whimpering. Lulu broke free, shaking the limp body of the dog in her mouth like a stuffed toy. A second dog scampered across the sand bar, yelping. More dogs rushed in. Caleb picked up a piece of driftwood and stood at the edges, pistol in left hand and flailing at the dogs.

The first bullet landed at his feet with a soft whump, spraying him with sand and gravel. The report sounded a second later, high pitched and hollow. A second bullet struck one of the dogs. The animal hobbled away crying, dragging a rear leg. The third bullet whined through the air past Caleb's head. Caleb dropped to a crouch and the pack swirled around him. "Get down," he yelled. Jessica didn't move. He couldn't see her face.

"Get down," he screamed, and she dropped to her knees.

More shots. Another dog hit.

"Run," Caleb yelled, but Jessica looked as planted as the cypress stump.

The shots from the bank multiplied. Close enough for muzzle flashes. Two people at least, maybe more. A high-powered deer rifle, and then eight or nine shots ratcheting off. An assault weapon. Bullets sprayed into the sand and overhead, all around the dogfight. Bad shots or just drunk, maybe not trying to kill anyone. There was barely enough light, but the sandbar glowed bright against the dark water and woods.

The wolves and dogs quieted. Confusion over the bullets falling around them, the noise of the guns, or just to catch their breaths before starting round two. The wolves stood panting side by side, at least four remaining dogs surrounding them. One dog lay on the beach a few feet away, crying and licking its wounds. Another dog lay dead, its throat ripped out by one of the wolves. The body of the first dog Caleb had shot lay thirty feet up the beach.

"Caleb?" Jessica called.

"You got people down here," Caleb yelled. "Quit your shooting."

"Hold your own goddamn shooting." Another spray of semi-automatic shots kicked up sand in front of the wolves.

Caleb shot the closest dog, hitting it in the chest and knocking it over. It lay quietly, dead. Caleb pointed at the next dog and shot again. It rolled over and over, yelping in pain.

"There's people down here goddammit," Caleb yelled.

"Fuck you, mister. That bitch of yours too."

The rifle shot whipped through the air past his head. Caleb aimed at the muzzle flash and fired another shot. A shotgun from behind Caleb. He heard buckshot rattling the trees where the men were shooting. Somebody—Hubert?—was somewhere behind him, too far away for the shotgun to be much use. Movement in the dark of the underbrush, someone cursed, and then a whispered conversation from the undergrowth. The shotgun again, a slug whistling overhead and toward the sound of the voices. Caleb crept over beside the two wolves and gathered the ends of their leashes and wrapped them a turn around his hand.

The wolves remained still, but one of the dogs moved toward them, letting out a low growl. Caleb shot the dog. The wolves exploded at the ends of their leashes, but he was able to hold onto them.

"Asshole," one of the voices said.

Caleb aimed at the voice and fired, and without waiting to see what happened next, pulled and dragged the wolves across the beach. Shots erupted from the woods. He found Jessica.

"Let's go," he whispered. "We got to get into the trees."

Jessica grabbed Lulu's lead. The last dog moved toward the wolves and Caleb shot it. He thought his clip might be empty. The spare clip was still on the beach somewhere.

"You're dead, asshole."

Hubert's shotgun sprayed the woods, much closer now. Caleb grabbed Jessica's arm and pulled. "Get out of here," Caleb yelled, hoping Hubert would hear. They dragged the wolves across the creek and scrambled up the opposite bank. "We're okay," he yelled. "Take care of yourself."

"You're a long way from okay, motherfucker." The voice from across the river was barely audible over the wind.

They got into a saw-briar thicket, the vines catching and ripping their clothes, tripping their feet, cutting their hands and faces. They crouched and waited. Caleb ejected the clip and thumbed the remaining bullets into the palm of his hand. Two bullets and one in the chamber. He'd shot nine times and killed a few dogs. He didn't think he'd shot a man. The woods were ripe with rain and mud, the wolves stank of blood and musk. The wind blew a hard storm across them, the air becoming water, blind with the dark and the rain. He reloaded the clip, going by feel, and shoved it into the handle of the gun.

Caleb wrapped the leashes around the trunk of a sapling to hold them, and the wolves settled down to lick their wounds. Their ears pricked at the sound of movement in the woods. Some splashing and cursing from the sandbar, and then the shotgun again. More automatic gunfire. Caleb wondered how many clips that asshole was carrying. Splashing and then just the sound of the rain, loud and drumming, consuming all other noise. He pulled Jessica close and held her. She was trembling. Complete darkness.

Hubert shot to cause confusion, cover for Caleb and Jessica to get away. It seemed forever for Caleb to get the wolves and Jessica off the beach and into the woods. The men came out of the woods slowly, slipped down a steep bank slick with the rain, and walked over to the sandbar and huddled over their dead and dying dogs, cursing. He held his gun over them the whole time, wondering if the first shell in the shotgun was buckshot or a slug. It would be nice to settle the trouble now, but it was too far for buckshot and the light was poor. He didn't want that asshole with the machine gun cutting loose.

Hubert couldn't believe his luck when the men split up and one of them came over to his bank and clambered up. He couldn't even tell what the man looked like, other than he had a ball cap and a beard, smelled of alcohol and sweat and dog, and he was carrying a rifle. The man grunted and stumbled like a drunk on Sunday morning. He was confused by the wind and the rain and wasn't too bright, because it took him forever to remember he had a flashlight. He clicked it on when he was two steps from where Hubert waited. The sudden light blinded Hubert. The man pointed it directly into his face as Hubert stepped forward.

The man got out, "What the fu-" before Hubert smashed his face with the butt of his shotgun. It was a good feeling. The man's teeth and jaw collapsed under the walnut. He sank to the ground like a tent with the poles pulled out. Hubert picked up the flashlight and switched it off and listened for the other two. The wind drowned out any other sound, but he saw flashes of light in the woods on the other side of the river. They were looking for Caleb and Jessica, or else lost. Hubert shielded the flashlight with his hand and switched it on. The man's face was a mess, starting to swell. Hubert had broken his jaw and messed up his teeth. He moaned a little and his eyes opened and widened. He tried to yell but couldn't do more than make a whistling sound that wouldn't carry over the wind. The man wore a sleeveless T-shirt and he'd disgraced God's temple with tattoos that ran wrist to shoulder. The man made a move to get up and Hubert smacked him in the temple with the flashlight. It was black and heavy and bright, four D cell batteries, as good as a hammer. He picked up the man's dropped rifle and looked at it, figuring out how it worked. It looked like the guns he'd seen on the news, rag-heads waving them around and shooting into the air in Iraq and Afghanistan. Hubert worked the gun until he could eject the clip. He rolled the man over and found a couple of fresh clips in his back pocket, along with his wallet. He put a fresh clip in the rifle and worked the slide to chamber a fresh round and switched the safety to S, then he bent down and picked up the ejected bullet and put it in his pocket. The storm broke over him, wind whipping and the rain coming in sheets. He sat down beside the man and opened his wallet and found twenty-three dollars and his drivers' license.

"Go to Hell Raymond Worley," Hubert said. He rapped Worley's head again with the flashlight, then slipped Worley's wallet back into his pocket and put the license into his own pocket, slung the rifle over his shoulder, and stood up. He pulled a few broken branches off the ground and covered the man, then went to look for his friends.

They put the wolves back into the pen and they went to ground in their den. Lulu had a cut on one shoulder and she was limping. Max's nose was slashed and had begun to swell, but neither wolf seemed to be hurt too badly. There were more shots from the woods. The shotgun pumped off five shells at once, and then a couple of isolated shots. More automatic fire, fading into the distance, and then quiet.

Caleb and Jessica struggled against the wind and rain as they walked to the house. Caleb loaded a .357 revolver and gave it to her. She didn't like guns, but she knew how to shoot. She took it like a hard fact. Caleb reloaded the nine millimeter and a couple of extra clips, then the twelve gauge pump and the sixteen gauge automatic. They went back into the night, feeling their way under the alternating bands of pouring rain and brief patches of moonlit open sky. He dropped Jessica at the wolf den, then worked back to the river, zig-zagging, looking for bodies where he thought they might be, finding nothing. He crossed the fence that marked Hubert's land and found tire tracks in the mud. It had been Hubert out that night.

The storm hit with intent to harm. The rain felt like a physical assault, bullying, relentless. Caleb gave up and went back for Jessica and the wind blew them off track as they stumbled trying to find their way home. Wind-driven rain made it impossible to look ahead, so Caleb navigated by memory, using a flashlight to try and stay on the trail. Dead pines fell and branches and pine needles whipped past their heads.

The wind shook the house so it rattled and creaked and moaned. Caleb imagined the house like a ship on the sea, riding out the storm. The electricity was down but Caleb started the generator, so they had enough power for the refrigerator, television, and a couple of lights. On the television, the radar showed bands of bright red sweeping over them, swirling out from the eye so the weather hit from the Southeast. The eye was making landfall in Louisiana, at the mouth of the Mississippi, and tracking eastward. One of the wolves howled above the sound of the wind, over the creaking pines and knocking branches. Caleb lit a gasoline lantern for extra light. The antenna went down in the wind and the television screen was just snow.

Jessica dressed their scratches. Her face looked old. Her shadow played across the walls. "Did you kill anyone?"

"I don't think so."

"Were you trying to kill them?"

"I'm not sure," Caleb said. "At the end, maybe so."

"That's what I thought."

Jessica made a pallet in the downstairs hallway between the bathroom and kitchen. She fell asleep quickly. Caleb felt exhaustion coming on, pushing the adrenaline out of his body like water filling a reservoir. A jittery pain ran down his leg. His fingers tingled. He needed to move. A vague sense of dread, the feeling that he was in trouble, that something bad was coming but he didn't know when or where or how bad it would really be. The storm lulled as Caleb got up and walked to the kitchen.

The shotgun lay on the kitchen table, beaded over with raindrops. He wiped it down with an oiled cloth out of the cabinet, then cradled it in his arms and went to the refrigerator and took out a beer and walked into the den and settled into the recliner with the shotgun across his lap. The rain and wind slammed into the house as a new storm band struck. He put fresh batteries into the weather band radio and tuned in the NOAH weather station, broadcasting live at two a.m. The hurricane had skimmed past New Orleans, missing it, but it was sliding up the coastline, following the curve north and east from Louisiana and into Mississippi. The outer bands of the hurricane filled the Eastern half of the Gulf of Mexico, from Louisiana to the Florida peninsula.

Caleb finished his beer. He called his father but got no answer. The lines were down now. He worried about the wolves but knew there was nothing he could do about that. He worried about Hubert. Whoever those assholes were, they wouldn't have sense enough to go home. They would be like the people partying on the coast whenever a hurricane hit, thinking they were bullet proof. They would be out there, protected by the patron saint of ignorant and mean-spirited men. He put on a raincoat and carrying the shotgun, went out to look for his father.

He hunched against the rain and the pine needles and leaves and branches whipping past, driven by the wind. He wiped the rain out of his eyes but couldn't clear them. Tree limbs cracked and groaned and splintered. Trees toppled in the woods and crashed. The raincoat puffed in the wind and he tried to pull it tighter. He pulled the hood over his ball cap but couldn't hear, so he pulled it off and stuffed it in his back pocket so the wind wouldn't blow it off his head. He strapped on the headlamp and leaned into the wind.

The wolves waited by the gate, skittish and pacing. Caleb leaned the shotgun against the chain link and opened the gate and slipped inside. Lulu whimpered and flattened on the ground, but it wasn't a submissive posture. She looked like a rattlesnake curled to strike. Max growled at him and backed away, disappeared into the darkness and reappeared behind him. He circled again. Caleb tried to pick him out of the dark, spinning. When the wolf hit him from behind, if felt like eighth grade football, when Clarence Horton, a running back who'd been held back two grades, steamrolled him as Caleb attempted a tackle. He went down, and the wolf stood over him with its teeth bared, throat rumbling. Caleb had never been afraid of Max before. He had made the mistake of treating the wolf like a huge dog, though he knew better.

Caleb lay in the mud with the wolf over him. Lulu crept closer, slung close to the ground, rumbling. He slowly raised one hand, intending to soothe the wolf standing over him, but Max tensed and snarled. Caleb imagined his father's words when they found the shreds of his body after the storm passed: "I tried to tell that boy about them wolves but he just wouldn't listen." People in the county who'd written letters would get a sense of satisfaction out of destroying the wolves, their fears justified. Caleb felt as bad as the day Jessica had left him, hurt that the wolves would turn against him, even in a hurricane. He looked up into the wolf's snarling mouth and exhaled, tried to make his body relax into a full submissive posture, and waited for whatever was going to happen next.

The pickup rocked in the wind, tilting like it might turn over before dropping back to the ground. Hubert wanted a cigarette, but his hands trembled too badly to roll one, and he couldn't catch his breath anyway. He pulled on the oxygen mask and opened the valve on the tank until he felt settled, then picked up his Bible off the seat and went back to reading, taking up where he had left off when the gunshots first sounded down by the river. He had been in the book of *Job*, his favorite part of the Bible, where God finally got tired of listening to everyone's whining and philosophizing about who He was and decided to sit everyone down and set them straight. He took up his place and started reading again:

Then the Lord answered Job out of the whirlwind, and said, Who is this that darkeneth counsel by words without knowledge? Gird up now thy loins like a man; for I will demand of thee, and Answer thou me.

Where wast thou when I laid the foundations of the earth? Declare, if thou hast understanding.

Who hath laid the measures thereof, if thou knowest? Or who hath stretched the line upon it?

Whereupon are the foundations thereof fastened? Or who laid the corner stone thereof?

Hast thou commanded the morn-
ing since thy days; and caused the day-
spring to know his place;
That it might take hold of the ends
of the earth, that the wicked might
be shaken out of it?

"Gird up thy loins like a man," Hubert thought. Fasten your damn britches and go out and face the world. He thought that it would make a good saying to have needle-pointed and hung on the wall, or carved into his headstone.

That was the beauty of the book. It was just as true now as it was the day God spoke it into existence. He could picture God shaking the earth like a salt shaker, sprinkling out the wicked like rats out of their holes. It was happening now, right there in Chickasaway County. The wicked were scurrying everywhere you looked: The papermill bastards dumping chemicals into the Neshoba, sitting back in their brick homes sipping their liquor and laughing at the poor people who couldn't even fish the river anymore; the hippies and lesbians and devil worshippers committing acts of perversion on cattle and each other; the men who had shot at his son—willful evil bastards who had the nerve to run their hounds across another man's land and then shoot at him. Hubert had been glad to see Caleb shooting back. He was glad the boy missed. He didn't want him to go to judgement and have to account for taking a human life.

He shook his head. Can't hit anything at night with a pistol. You need a shotgun. Even the son of a bitch with a machine gun couldn't find his ass with both hands. Smashing that man's face had felt like redemption.

> *Hast thou entered into the springs of the sea? or hast thou walked in the search of the depth? Have the gates of death been opened unto thee?*
> *or hast thou seen the doors of the shadow of death?*
> *Hast thou perceived the breadth of the earth? Declare if thou knowest it all.*

Hubert put the book down, feeling its weight magnify. He struggled to lift the book off his lap, and when he lay it on the seat of the pickup, it fell to the floor like an invisible hand had knocked it off. The storm shook the pickup and rain hammered the roof like an impact wrench. He struggled to breathe and panicked, fumbling for the oxygen mask and trying to open the valve. He wondered when he had become so clumsy that turning a valve required all his concentration. His body floated off the seat and he gripped the steering wheel with his free hand. The dashboard blurred and he turned off the interior cab light. He tried to breathe but it felt like the oxygen tank was empty. He wanted to tell God that he was ready to be taken, but he knew that wasn't true. He was afraid to die, and there was lingering unfinished business. He prayed: "I'm weak and sinful, Lord, just like everyone else. You know that. But I'd like to see this business with Caleb cleared up. He's lost and confused, and he's drifted away from You. I know there's something I can say to him, though. If you'll just allow me to place a drop of water on his

234 - TERRY ENGEL

tongue, I know I can save him from torment. You can do what you like to me. Just let me save my boy."

He felt better with the prayer. The oxygen cleared his vision and he felt his body weight returning, his strength growing. The boy needs help, Hubert kept thinking.

That was when he saw the men, three of them, two holding guns and carrying the third between them. His anger returned like a tire inflated by a weak compressor, slowly filling and rounding out the rubber until it was fully shaped and ready to be mounted.

He watched the men come closer, crossing his land, bold as bold. His land where he'd run cattle most of his life. They were mean men, and he knew that after the storm, they'd come back and kill Caleb, kill his wife, even kill the damn wolves. It was all he could do to not roll a cigarette, but didn't want his hands occupied when the shooting started nor the smoke to drive him into a fit of coughing.

He cranked the truck and shifted into drive and gunned the truck across the pasture, freezing the men in his highbeams. He stopped in front of them. The men just stood there as he opened the door and stepped down, pulling the assault rifle after him.

"We ain't doing nothing," one of the men yelled. "Just trying to get back to our truck."

As Hubert switched the gun off safety, the two men dropped their friend and tried to level their own guns. Hubert pulled the trigger and emptied the clip. He stared for a long time at what he had done, then pulled himself back into his truck and closed his eyes while the storm rolled over him.

She woke and sensed she was alone, though there was no reason to believe this. In her dream, she had ran through the maze of woods, looking for Caleb but not finding him. She sat up and assured herself that she was safe. The wind rocked the house; she listened for the wolves, listened for Caleb. She reached for her flashlight and got out of bed and pulled on a denim shirt, went downstairs and found him gone. She wondered if something had happened, if the men had come back. She replayed the night, the whistle of the bullets, the screaming dogs, the way Caleb turned his pistol on the dogs so easily. In the briar thickets cowering like a hunted rabbit. Panic rising, pushing at the inside of her face like lava in a volcano. The relief of coming home. The house had never felt so safe before.

I've got to be tougher than this, she thought, wandering back to her bedroom. But it shouldn't be this difficult. Nothing had prepared her for firefights in her own woods, not even the welder's strike at the shipyard when the scabs had tried to cross the line and she had picked out a man in the opposing line smaller than her. The men around her held baseball bats, chains, lengths of pipe. She'd brought nothing other than her anger. Luckily, the scabs had backed down, but she wondered what she would have done if they'd pressed the picket line.

Caleb should have been able to stop it from happening. She truly believed this, even though she couldn't think what he could have done different. He had a way of diffusing trouble, not over-reacting. But the idea worked through, guilting her.

She slipped into a pair of jeans and boots. The flashlight pointed away from her where it lay on the bed, casting odd shadows on the wall. Her bag was in the closet. She'd never fully unpacked when she came home. She opened it and tried to think what she needed to put in it. She moved around the room filling it with whatever of hers came to hand, trying not to think about what she was doing. Once through the room and she was done. She looked at her bedroom and thought about seeing it for the last time. Deja vu rolled over her, making her remember the last time she'd packed a bag. The .357 lay on her bedside table. She'd brushed it with her fingers but left it. Where the hell was Caleb? It nagged at her, the guilt flying over her like the way she felt when her mother used to nag her about smoking, her lies. She walked downstairs and sat on the couch. The radio talked about the storm in a mechanical voice, giving the data about wind speeds, precipitation, barometric pressure, a long list of counties under severe storm warning, what to do to prepare for the hell that was breaking all over the south end of the state and would only get worse. Her legs crawled with imaginary insects under her skin. She rubbed them but the feeling wouldn't go away. She stood up and started toward the door. She stopped at the memory of their first real fight, though she couldn't remember what it had been about. Something minor. Something stupid. She had stormed out the door and climbed into her Subaru, ready to drive away. He had followed, and as she put the car in reverse, he had slashed the sidewall of the front passenger tire with his pocketknife. She stopped and climbed out.

He looked stupid holding his knife like he was getting ready to fight. He realized it, looking at the opened blade, and folded it and put it in his back pocket, looking like a little boy caught looking at the lingerie ads in the Sunday paper.

She bent down to look at her tire, stuck her finger in the slit. "Goddammit, Caleb."

He stuck his hands in his back pockets. "I may have overreacted," he said, looking ashamed. He wouldn't look at her. He looked at the tire.

"Maybe we both did."

"I just know that I won't sleep and you won't sleep. So we might as well make up now and save ourselves the trouble of doing it later." He looked off at something. "Or at least talk about it more."

She couldn't explain why she had gone back inside with him that time. Maybe the fight had been stupid. Maybe it was because it was something that her father would have done, and she had never seen that side of Caleb.

Once inside, whatever they had argued about had been forgotten. Caleb said, "I don't want to be like my father." At the time she hadn't known Hubert well enough to fully understand what he meant.

Jessica went into the kitchen for water. Supper dishes from the night before stood in the sink. As she drank she studied the dishes, then went to the sink and placed the stopper in the drain, squirted in some dish soap, and ran hot water, only it wasn't very hot since the power was out. She put a pot of water onto the gas burner of the stove and lit a lantern to save her flashlight battery. She watched the water steam to

238 ~ TERRY ENGEL

a boil, thinking about nothing, thinking about everything. Only a fraction of her life had been lived in this
house, a little more than a quarter, but it was the part
that she most wanted to hold on to at this moment.
She had tried moving on and hadn't liked it. Hadn't
liked what she had become, or the way other people
looked at her. She wasn't a quitter.

The water bubbled and she poured it into the
sink and mixed in a little cold. The warm water felt
good on her arms. Her fingers were stiff and sore from
holding fists all night. She liked the motion of running
a cloth over the plates and glasses. It was satisfying
to have dishes sanitized by hot water, a mechanical
action. It was like welding, a combination of chemistry
and physics and a steady hand. She rinsed the clean
dishes and stacked them into the drainboard, steam
evaporating off them.

When she finished she looked up at the clock and
wondered if it was right. It didn't seem that late, but
the clock ran on batteries. Caleb had been gone a long
time. Something must have happened. She went upstairs for the pistol and tucked it into the waist of her
jeans. She pulled on her rain jacket and hurried out
the door.

She leaned into the wind. Debris whipped through
her flashlight beam, briefly lit like shooting stars
streaking across a dark sky. She was surprised to find
the gate to the pen open. Caleb sat in the mud.

"What happened?" she yelled. "Did they come
back?"

He just sat there, holding one hand in the other.
She saw it was bleeding, a long gash across the back.
His tan skin blanched white under the flashlight beam
and he turned away from the too sudden light.

She turned it away and knelt in the mud beside him, wrapping the arm with the flashlight around him and touching his hand.

"Max went crazy with the storm. They both did. They're gone. She felt a surge of sick. She shined the light around the pen, looking for Max and Lulu, letting his words sink in.

They looked for the wolves; they looked for Hubert. But the storm fell on them with something that felt like the end of time, the end of the world, and ultimately they turned back to the house to save their own lives, wading and even swimming in the low spots, crawling when they could no longer walk, blinded by rain and wind-swept debris, only finding their way home because they had found their way home so many times in the dark, and they knew the contours of the land like the text of a favorite and often read book.

The house rocked in the winds and shuddered with each tree that fell on it. Candles and lantern light flickered and cast weird shadows. Jessica started out to crank the generator, but Caleb told her it was better to save the gas. It would be days, maybe weeks, before they got power back. The rain rattled the windows and siding like handfuls of thrown gravel. Water stains spread across the ceilings. Caleb lay on the couch, the last of the ice from the freezer wrapped in a dish towel and around his hand. He turned off the weather radio, sick of the redundancy. Toward morning the sky glowed with a weak yellow light in the east. The winds and sound subsided as the eye passed over. The quiet lasted for maybe twenty minutes before the back wall hit. Jessica curled with Caleb on the couch, too tired to care much about whatever was going to happen next. She tried to worry out loud about the wolves, but Caleb shook his head and said "Let's not talk about it."

As the day wore on the rotation of the storm bands spun off tornados. The light stayed the same yellow dog color, no brighter at noon than it had been at sunrise. Not long after noon a large section of the roof came off. Jessica poured out the last of the coffee left in the pot from the day before and pulled two lukewarm beers out of the refrigerator. She handed one to Caleb, who pulled the top and clicked cans with her, said "Easy come, easy go." She tried to smile and failed.

Caleb finished his beer and went to the kitchen for another. Outside the pines lay about the house at all angles, the limbs broken and rocking limply in the breeze. The ground was littered with branches, leaves, trash, shingles, plywood, and sheets of metal. The storm appeared to be lifting at times, though another band soon followed. Caleb told Jessica that he figured the only thing holding the house together was all the trees fallen onto it. Jessica just looked at the house coming apart all around her. She looked like she did the morning after the baby died.

Just before dark a thin ray of sunset cast an orange glow that filled the room through a hole in the ceiling before it burned down to maroon and finally darkness. They got off the couch where they'd fallen asleep together as the storm wound down. Jessica opened the cabinets and stared at the cans and pasta like she'd never cooked before. Caleb thought about how on any other day he'd be feeding the wolves, thinking about a walk and a swim. He ran an oiled cloth over the pistols again and checked the loads, making sure there were no cartridges in the chambers. He took down a rifle from the gun-rack, loaded it, and filled his pocket with cartridges. He laced up his boots. Jessica pulled on her boots and took the pistol when he offered.

"Is there any chance we'll find them?"

Caleb shook his head.

Outside, the world seemed incredibly green in the light of the flashlights. The air was aromatic with pine. What grass had been left from the drought glistened wet and green with the rain. The pine forest had collapsed on the house and the yard, an obstacle course of barriers and walls to climb over or crawl through. Going around wouldn't solve any problems.

Caleb flashed the light over his pickup. All the windows busted out and the cab crushed under a tree trunk. Jessica's Subaru was hemmed in by fallen trees, but it seemed to have little damage. It would take a lot of work to clear it out. The driveway looked like someone had emptied a tin of Lincoln Logs onto the floor. The house had a furrow plowed through the roof and two-thirds of the top floor. It canted at a bad angle, and Caleb thought the only solution was to knock it down with the bulldozer and start fresh. He was surprised to not feel anything.

He looked at Jessica, who had clambered over to her car and had brushed back some limbs and opened the door and looked inside. She was smiling.

"You care more about that car than you do the house."

She smiled. "I've had the car longer."

They started toward the wolf pen out of habit, but the trail was buried under fallen timber. Caleb's woods were a no-man's land of broken and splintered tree trunks. The ground was soaked and when they weren't picking a path across trees they slipped and slogged through mud. A few of the thinner pines were lain down, but they would spring back eventually. The pulp-wooders would have their pick of woods to clean up and sell, but there would be so much pulp Indian River--assuming it still stood--could cut prices to nothing and make enough paper to cover the moon. They struggled to the top of the ridge and paused to catch their breath.

They dropped off the ridge down to the creek, finding the water out of its banks and filling the woods for a couple hundred yards across. Any evidence from the shooting the night before would be swept away. They crossed the line to Hubert's land and kept going beyond the cornfields, finding the going much easier.

After the corn there would be another stand of woods, pastures, then the road, then Hubert's house.

When they got to the woods Caleb stopped to listen. Barking, and just beneath the sound of the barking, the bawling of anxious cattle. He looked at Jessica. She heard it too. They started into the woods.

Caleb stopped at the edge of Hubert's pasture and listened. The cattle were spooked, but there was a buzzing undercurrent he couldn't identify, like a disturbed hornet nest. The air smelled sweet from the wet round black bales of hay spaced across the field. There was a dark shape on the ground about a hundred yards away. The shape pulsed, moving like the chest of a giant breathing.

"Wait here," he said, and eased up on the shape, trying to be quiet. The ground was wet and the hay stubble soft under his boots. He knew what it was, but he was afraid to admit it.

The cow was down. Max had the cow by the throat, tugging. Lulu backed away from the cow's torn belly, her head low to the ground and her hackles up, growling at him. The smell was foul—worse than a butchered cow should smell. Max growled then. He eased toward Caleb, head low and tail switching.

"They didn't kill it," Jessica said. She was close enough behind Caleb to make him jump.

Caleb didn't know what to say.

"I want to see what happened to it," Jessica said. She was shaking.

"Let me look first," Caleb said. "I've never seen them like this."

He walked up to the cow. Max and Lulu backed off a few steps, sprang around and ran away and stopped, then crept forward again. Low pitched growls, deep inside, shook Caleb enough to pull his pistol out of his jeans and chamber a round. He knelt by the cow and looked it over. He shook off the memory. There was a bulge low, distorting the shape under the hind legs. A breech calf. Caleb lay his pistol on the ground, took off his jacket, and rolled a shirt sleeve. When he stuck his arm inside the cow it was warm and tight. He touched something hard and pointed, a hoof, and when he moved up he felt the hind leg, turned the wrong way. He pulled his arm out and picked up his pistol and backed toward Jessica. Max and Lulu moved between him and the cow, staring hard, their tails switching.

He told Jessica what he had found. "She didn't' stand a chance without someone to help her."

Lulu began to slink toward them and they backed off. Max took the cow's throat in his mouth and shook it like it didn't weigh anything. Lulu broke off and ran a wide circle around the cow before dashing in and ripping at the stomach and hindquarters.

"Leave it alone," Jessica yelled.

Caleb tried to think of some way to get Max and Lulu back to the pen. With Max and Lulu wild, would they be able to come back? Hubert had to be dead, or hurt. He wouldn't leave a birthing cow in the field if he could walk or crawl. Caleb was almost relieved when from the far end of the field, a truck came out of the trees and started a circuit inside the fence, toiling in four wheel drive through the saturated ground, slinging mud. A spotlight swept back and forth from the truck, lighting the round bales of hay. Caleb smiled, imagining his father in the cab, a hand rolled dangling from his lips, shotgun propped against the seat, counting his cattle. Whatever happened now, Caleb knew, would happen fast.

He would have to get the shotgun away from his father before he figured out what was happening. The truck took forever to circuit the pasture. Max and Lulu worked on the cow, moving with a natural grace and disturbing intensity. It was terrible to watch, and beautiful.

Jessica kneeled on the wet ground on one side of the cow. The spotlight danced toward them, flashed past, and came back and centered on the cow. Caleb shielded his eyes from the glare as the pickup turned toward them and pulled to a stop a few yards off.

The headlights and spotlight drowned everything but the cow and the wolves. Max dropped the cow's neck and crouched beside the body. His eyes glowed red in the headlights. Lulu dropped to the ground behind the cow, hackles raised, growling as Hubert stepped out of the truck holding the shotgun.

"I told you I'd kill those damn wolves."

"Hold on Hubert," Caleb said, his arms wide.

Hubert raised his shotgun and shot Max. The wolf flipped over once and lay still, whimpering. Lulu cowered for a moment, then slinked around the cow and started toward Hubert, snarling. He tried to pump another shell in, but he was too clumsy and weak to work the shotgun and it jammed. Lulu moved closer, ready to pounce.

Hubert looked up from his shotgun. He gave the wolf a hateful stare and tried to claw the jammed shell out of the chamber.

Caleb aimed his pistol at Lulu, tracking her.

Lulu closed to within a few feet of Hubert, paused as if questioning whether it was right to attack a man, and gathered herself.

As she leaped Caleb squeezed the trigger. Lulu hit Hubert and he went down, the wolf in his lap, dying. Caleb shot again and the wolf settled, collapsing onto Hubert like a boat sinking beneath the surface. Hubert sat on the ground holding the wolf's head in his hands and staring at Caleb.

Caleb went to his father and kneeled down beside him. He placed one hand on Hubert's shoulder, took one of his hands in his own. It felt strange to touch his father; they'd touched so rarely over their long history.

"They didn't kill it," Caleb said.

"What?"

Hubert looked confused, and Caleb didn't know if he was still in the world or not.

Jessica went to Hubert's other side and kneeled, her hands in her lap. Hubert wheezed. He looked at the two of them with wild eyes. His hat had fallen off and his bald head made him look like a wild bird. Caleb realized that he would have to bury his father with a hat.

Hubert fell back on the hay stubble and his breathing stopped.

Jessica patted the old man, once, twice, three times, then stood up and went over to Max. She sat on the ground and pulled the wolf's head into her lap and ran her fingers through his fur. Caleb watched her for a moment, then looked down at his father. He looked very still and pale and at peace; all the anger had finally leaked out of him. Caleb couldn't imagine a world without his father any more than Hubert could have imagined a world without God. With the night quiet and the wolves dead, the cows crowded the truck and bawled for food. Caleb stood and walked back to the cow and stared at it, then he turned and looked at Jessica. She was smoothing Max's fur and Caleb watched her in the headlights.

He wondered where they would go from here. He remembered a day long ago when they'd first started dating. They'd gone for a drive down to the coast—Jessica wanted to show Caleb where she'd grown up—and they'd ended up a little lost and following signs for a state park. They'd driven through thick woods separated by canals bordered by tall, sand colored grass, then turned onto another road that led through a subdivision where the houses backed up to a fifty-foot wide channel. They stopped on a bridge spanning the waterway. The back yards were trucked in topsoil planted with carpets of thick grass, held up by concrete and cross tie retaining walls. There was a thin strip of mud between the base of the walls and the water's edge, spanned by piers that ran into the canal with every kind of boat tied to the end: canoes, jet skis, bass boats, sailboats, and cabin cruisers.

The park headquarters were in a mobile home painted rustic brown, and the only other building was a pavilion that covered three picnic tables and a pair of restrooms, but there were no cars anywhere. A sign with the symbol for a boat launch stamped into the wood pointed down a long, straight dirt road. Hundreds, maybe thousands of tiny crabs scuttled across the road, which was flanked by palmetto and pine and foot high fire ant mounds. The road ended in a circle turn-around with a dirt ramp down to the canal. A wooden pier extended into the water. A mini-van with roof rack was parked in front of the dock. They parked and sat on the end of the pier and dangled their legs above the water, watching a gray-haired couple paddle toward them in a two-seater kayak. The woman raised one hand and waved as they coasted into the landing. Caleb went over to steady the boat as they climbed out and stood in ankle deep water.

The woman was attractive, her face colored from exercise and the sun. She was barefoot and wore a straw hat with a scarf tied around the brim. The ends of the scarf flowed across her shoulders. Her jeans were rolled up on her ankles. The man looked healthy, one of those old guys who still ran and played racquetball and would live to be a hundred. Jessica chatted with them about some of the places she camped as a teenager. Caleb talked boats with the man, told him about canoeing Black Creek. The kayak was fiberglass. He picked up one end and tested the weight and was surprised by its lightness.

"Give it a try," the man said.

The woman held the boat steady while they climbed in and got settled, Jessica in the front and Caleb in back. It was more stable than Caleb expected. They paddled back and forth in front of the pier, and then Jessica pointed in the direction that the couple had paddled from.

The water was thick with algae just below the surface, but the kayak floated right over it. The channel narrowed, crabs scuttled into the water from the mud banks, and small catfish skipped through the water, flying short distances.

After a few hundred yards Jessica stopped. She lay her paddle across the gunwale and pointed. An eight-foot alligator sunned on a bank thirty yards away. The mud bank was smooth from animals sliding into the water. The alligator raised its head a couple of inches and the skin of its throat moved as it breathed. They watched for several minutes. Jessica corrected the boat with her paddle every so often.

"I wonder what they sound like," Jessica said.

"Like lions."

"I believe it."

The alligator moved into the water, placing each foot deliberately in small steps, sliding forward until just the eyes and nostrils showed, and then it sank out of sight. They paddled backwards until they got the kayak turned in the right direction, then headed back. They paddled around the bend and saw the old couple standing on the pier. The woman waved and Jessica waved back. Caleb stopped paddling and the kayak slewed off to one side. Jessica put down her paddle and looked back at him.

"That was something," she said.

She moved her paddle through the water, a tentative stroke, and then she smiled. Her face lit up like a child seeing something wonderful for the first time—a bird flying through the air or a dancer twirling in endless pirouette, or a wolf loping as gracefully as flowing water across an open field.

Now, Jessica looked up at Caleb and smiled again. This time it was a sad smile, a broken smile, a smile offered because no other response was adequate, and it was just easier to smile. A smile that concentrated the sadness of the world, the difficulty of the past few years, all the fear and doubt and frustration and anger. A tired, wrung-out, drained, empty, exhausted smile. An I give up smile. She smiled at Caleb because it seemed that he was the only one who could possibly know what she was feeling, what she had lost, what they had been through. It seemed to Caleb that she smiled because they were starting over from nothing, except for each other.

Maybe that was enough.

Caleb nodded back at Jessica, his lips pulled thin in the same smile

My God, he thought. She was beautiful.

Acknowledgements

I want to thank my colleagues in the English Department at Harding University for their friendship and support, and in particular, I am deeply grateful to Paulette Guerin for her encouragement, editorial advice and keen proofreader's eye on this and other projects.

I look back fondly at my time in the writing program at the University of Southern Mississippi, which transformed me in so many ways that I can't begin to address them all. Suffice it to say that I left Hattiesburg a much different, and better, person than I arrived. I am especially grateful to Frederick Barthelme and Steven Barthelme, who challenged me, who offered advice and support, and who are still in my head every time I sit down to write. Thank you to Rie Fortenberry, the glue that held the Center for Writers together; to Kim Herzinger, who taught me to "like as much as I can"; to Angela Ball, who taught me about rhythms of language; and to Melanie Hendricks, Andy Plattner, Jim Whorton, Kevin Walters, Caroline Prince, John Fleming, and my other friends at the Center for Writers who helped me along the way.

I am thankful to my parents, Clarence and Peggy Engel, who both taught me the value of hard work and faith. I thank my father, who first taught me to love woods and water, a legacy I try to pass down to my children.

Most of all, I am grateful to my wife Lisa, and to my daughters Julia Rose and Stella, for their love and support and the joy that you bring me.

Credits

Portions of the text were originally published in slightly different form in the following:

"Max and Lulu" in *Product*;
Honorable Mention in *Pushcart Prize*

"Blizzard," "Night Walking along Black Creek," and "Coyotes" in *Cave Region Review*

"Debris" in *The Sun Magazine*

A Mississippi native, Terry Engel grew up dreaming of
white-water rivers and mountains, and he has traveled
widely and lived in Colorado and Alaska. However,
his fiction and nonfiction continually wander back to
the slow rhythms of the South—Mississippi, Alabama,
Tennessee and Arkansas—back to the foothills of the
Appalachians, deep pine and bottomland hardwood
forests, open pastureland and fields, tannin stained
and cypress lined creeks, and its people.

Engel studied Forest Resources at Mississippi
State University and worked as quality control and
production supervisor in particleboard mills and wood
preservative treatment plants. He was a lineman for
the Tennessee Valley Authority, building high voltage
powerlines, and he has held other jobs selling books,
suppressing fires for the Mississippi Forestry Commis-
sion, building trails, working assembly lines, painting houses, and delivering exotic birds to pet stores.
He earned a Ph.D. in writing from the University of
Southern Mississippi, where he studied at the Center
for Writers with Frederick and Steven Barthelme and
Mary Robison. His work has appeared in a number of
literary journals and magazines, and he has received
the Transatlantic Review Award, won the Hemingway

Days Short Story Writing Contest, and received honorable mention from *Pushcart Prize*.

Currently, Engel teaches creative writing and literature at Harding University in Arkansas. He lives in Searcy with his wife and two children and a variety of animals.